QUICK REFERENCE FOR BAND DIRECTORS WHO TEACH ORCHESTRA

QUICK REFERENCE FOR BAND DIRECTORS WHO TEACH ORCHESTRA

Ronald E. Kearns

Published in cooperation with the
National Association for Music Education

Rowman & Littlefield
Lanham • Boulder • New York • London

Published in cooperation with the National Association for Music Education, 1806 Robert Fulton Drive, Reston, Virginia 20191, U.S.A.; nafme.org

Published by Rowman & Littlefield
A wholly owned subsidiary of The Rowman & Littlefield Publishing Group, Inc.
4501 Forbes Boulevard, Suite 200, Lanham, Maryland 20706
www.rowman.com

Unit A, Whitacre Mews, 26-34 Stannary Street, London SE11 4AB, United Kingdom

Copyright © 2020 by Ronald E. Kearns

All rights reserved. No part of this book may be reproduced in any form or by any electronic or mechanical means, including information storage and retrieval systems, without written permission from the publisher, except by a reviewer who may quote passages in a review.

British Library Cataloguing in Publication Information Available

Library of Congress Cataloging-in-Publication Data
ISBN 978-1-4758-5340-7 (cloth : alk. paper)
ISBN 978-1-4758-5341-4 (pbk. : alk. paper)
ISBN 978-1-4758-5342-1 (electronic)

To my late wife Lillie B. Kearns,
my biggest supporter and friend

Contents

Foreword	xi
Acknowledgments	xiii
Introduction	1

1 I'm a Band Teacher, and Now I Have to Teach Orchestra? ... 3
   Getting Started ... 3
   How Do I Start? ... 4
   The Importance of Using the Correct Bowing Terms to Describe How a Note Should Be Played ... 5
   On-String Bowing Techniques ... 6
   Off-the-String Bowing Techniques ... 6
   Playing without the Bow ... 8
   Playing Multiple Notes On the String or Off the String ... 9
   Bow Pressure on the String ... 10
   Vibrato on String Instruments ... 10
   Chapter at a Glance ... 12

2 Building a String Program in Your School or Strengthening an Existing One ... 13
   First Steps for Building a New String Program ... 13
   Developing Your Personal Philosophy of Music Education ... 14

	Creating a Support Network	15
	Planning for Your First Rehearsal	17
	Chapter at a Glance	18
3	**Creating a Syllabus and Orchestra Handbook**	**19**
	Grading Policies	19
	Developing a Handbook for Your Orchestra	20
	Program Description	22
	A Sample Orchestra Handbook	22
	Chapter at a Glance	25
4	**Writing Lesson Plans**	**27**
	Planning Lessons	27
	Here Are Some Sample Lesson Plans	28
	Sample Plan #1	28
	Sample Plan #2	29
	Sample Plan #3	30
	Sample Plan #4	33
	Chapter at a Glance	34
5	**Creating a Parent Group and Support System**	**35**
	Developing a Support System for Your Orchestra	35
	Establishing a New Parent Group	35
	Leadership Function	37
	Forming Committees	39
	Chapter at a Glance	40
6	**Literature Selection and the First Rehearsal**	**41**
	First Rehearsal	42
	Organizing the First Rehearsal and Classroom Management	43
	Ending the First Rehearsal	45
	Suggested Composers	45
	Suggested String Methods and Publishers	46
	Suggested Literature for Orchestra	47
	Chapter at a Glance	52

7 Having a Successful First Performance — 53
The Importance of a Successful First Performance — 53
Planning for a Successful First Performance — 53
First Performance Procedures — 55
Stage Entrance and Seating — 55
Performance Etiquette — 56
Carrying Instruments Going On Stage and
  Leaving the Stage — 57
Concertmaster Tuning on Stage — 57
Folder Uniformity and Performance Attire — 58
Chapter at a Glance — 59

8 Festival Preparation and Performance — 61
Festival Performance Planning — 61
Festival Information and Description — 61
Preparing to Be Adjudicated — 62
Score Study — 63
Make Notes on the Score — 63
Teaching the Music for Adjudication — 63
Record Your Rehearsals — 67
Chapter at a Glance — 68

9 Program Maintenance — 69
Maintaining Your Program — 69
Developing a Five-Year Plan — 69
Maintaining Equipment and Equipment Purchases — 70
The Importance of Individual Recognition and Praise — 73
Chapter at a Glance — 74

10 Using Technology in the Orchestra Classroom — 77
Using Technology as an Integral Part of Instruction — 77
Recording Your Group — 78
Using Tablets and Smartphones — 82
  Music on a Tablet — 82
Interactive Software — 83
Websites — 84
Social Media — 84

Facebook	84
Twitter	85
Google	85
Notation Software	85
Choosing the Best Notation Software for Your Program	86
Using Play-Along Software and Hardware	87
PowerPoint	88
Videotaping Your Orchestra	88
Technology Resources on the Internet	90
Maintenance and Record-Keeping	90
Teaching Resources in Book Form	91
Chapter at a Glance	91
11 Using Small Ensembles to Improve Your Orchestra's Sound	**93**
Small Ensembles	93
Using Solos to Keep Your Best Players Interested in Staying	95
Basic Small Ensemble Playing	97
Chapter at a Glance	98
Appendix A	**99**
Glossary	**103**
References	**105**
Index	**107**
About the Author	**115**

Foreword

Many of the strongest string teachers I have met in my forty-plus years in the field are by training wind and percussion players who have embraced the orchestra as a most serious medium of music education. Their orchestral ensembles stand equal to their wind and percussion groups in quality and in importance in their overall music programs. The commonality they all share is that all are first and foremost fine musicians.

I have known Ron Kearns for over thirty years as a fellow high school instrumental music teacher, most of those from my years in the Montgomery County, Maryland, school system. A product of Knoxville College and the Catholic University of America, Ron, an exemplary artist on the saxophone, has had demonstrated success teaching high school marching, symphonic and jazz band, and specifically for this book, string and symphony orchestra. Partway through his career, Ron was thrust into a high-pressure orchestra program where his natural curiosity for learning how to do things and then teach, coupled with his superb musicianship, brought him success as a band director teaching orchestra. Ron has a knowledge of instructional techniques and orchestral literature that makes his suggestions contained in this book valuable. Having "walked the walk," Ron lights the way for the band director faced with teaching strings through this book. There are more than a few band directors who have had a woefully insufficient string techniques class, or had that class so many years ago, that not much is remembered beyond the title of what was played on a final exam.

There are many challenges confronting a band director teaching strings. First and foremost, there is the imparting of correct instruction of string instrument playing techniques and principles of string ensemble playing, both as an independent group as in a string orchestra, or as a part of a symphony orchestra. These principles are similar to those used in band, but in some significant ways, different. Ron's book is filled with explanations and photographs that clarify these. This book is also filled with helpful information unique to a string program, such as creating an independent parent booster group, scheduling concerts independently of the band, creating an atmosphere of specialness, and ensuring that string students feel as important as band students. There are also chapters on how to plan rehearsals, prepare for adjudication, create chamber ensembles within a program, record an ensemble, and use technology to further student attainment of skills and musicianship. There is a helpful glossary of terms unique to string playing.

It is hoped that this book will prove a useful tool as you as a band director learn to become a strong and effective teacher of strings as well as band.

Bill Hollin

Music Director,
the Potomac Valley Youth Orchestra,
Montgomery County, Maryland
Lead Instrumental Music Teacher and
Head Director of Band and Orchestra Ensembles,
the Barbara Ingram School for the Arts,
Hagerstown, Maryland

Acknowledgments

When I wrote my first book I said that if you see a turtle on a fence post you know it didn't get there by itself. That was the case with my first two books, and the same is true with this one. Most of this book reflects lessons learned in my classrooms over thirty years of teaching. My orchestra students and students in the DC Youth Orchestra program taught me how to be a successful orchestra director.

My wife Lillie was supportive of my quest to learn the skills I needed to learn to become an orchestra director since I had never played in an orchestra. My daughter Tiffany Kearns had to become an orchestra director after being trained as a band director and at her first festival/assessment received straight Superior ratings. Many of the things included here are from a first-year teacher's viewpoint thanks to her. Along with Josalyn Walker, Tiffany shared quite a few insights into teaching students in the twenty-first century.

I want to thank Caroline Arlington of the National Association for Music Education who helped facilitate the publishing of this book. She was there for me whenever I reached out for assistance. While doing a clinic for Jeff Johns, a band director teaching orchestra, I casually mentioned that I was considering writing a book for band directors teaching orchestra. He said to me that based on my first book, *Quick Reference for Band Directors*, this book would fill a void.

There's a group for music teachers on Facebook where the music teaching community shares information to help each other. I asked for suggestions on orchestra music for teachers trying to establish an orchestra program. Lauren Scott sent me a list of "go-to" composers. Scott Krijnen gave me a list of composers and compositions by the grade level he had prepared for the California Music Educators Association.

Lauren is the wife of my longest-sitting concertmaster, Benjamin Scott, National Symphony Orchestra, who provided photographs to demonstrate proper string playing positions. Ben was concertmaster when my orchestra, became a Grade Six (highest grade level) full orchestra and we used a lot of the techniques discussed here to achieve that level of excellence.

I want to thank Stephanie Richards of Conn-Selmer for providing pictures from the Conn-Selmer catalog showing violins, violas, cellos, and basses. One phone call, and the next day I had everything I needed.

Last but certainly not least, I'd like to thank Rowman & Littlefield and NAfME for publishing this book. Their dedication to assisting music educators is unmatched.

Introduction

The purpose of this book is to assist band directors in the transition of becoming band and orchestra directors. It's also written to help instrumental teachers who have had little or no experience teaching orchestra become successful orchestra teachers. As a saxophonist, all of my ensemble experiences came from participation in bands and band satellite ensembles. After teaching band only, I took a job in Montgomery County, Maryland, and taught orchestra classes for twenty years.

The first thing I had to do was find classes that taught string pedagogy and orchestra conducting. I had two months to prepare. Unfortunately, during my first year, most of what I learned came from trial and error and helpful students. I discovered that the first thing I had to learn was orchestral terminology. Most of that terminology was related to bowing. As a band director I knew that good sound production was related to airflow through the wind instruments. Since orchestras depend on string instruments, sound production depends on string vibration. This meant that I needed to know about bowing and bow placement on the string. I got a violin and bow and practiced.

What I hope to do in this book is help you bridge the gap between band and orchestra teaching. String students are very different from band students. I discovered that there's a level of seriousness that string students possess that's very different from band students. Understanding these differences will help you reach these students.

As a "band person" you share a common bond with your band students. You sat where they're sitting. Converting to orchestra, you may feel like the proverbial fish out of water. It is the goal of this book to help make you feel more comfortable making the adjustment from band teacher to orchestra teacher. I will guide you through the process as a band director who successfully made the transition.

By the time I retired, my orchestras consistently received Superior ratings at festivals/assessments, never got less than third place in any national or international competition, and most importantly to me, in twenty years, never got less than a Superior rating in sight-reading. We played Grade Six literature, and my last full orchestra had eighty-three students.

Even though things worked out well over the years, I'm writing this book to help you to avoid the anxiety I went through in my early years. You'll notice that I constantly refer to you as a band or orchestra teacher. That's because I want you to realize that's what you are, a teacher first; conducting and directing are a result of good teaching.

1

I'm a Band Teacher, and Now I Have to Teach Orchestra?

Getting Started

As a band director who has been hired to teach band and orchestra, your first question may be, "How can I do this? I'm a band teacher, and now I have to teach orchestra?" The answer to this question is simple: learn new skills. Learn how to teach string students and learn how to communicate with them using the terms that are unique to strings. This may mean finding a string pedagogy course to take, learning how to play a string instrument, watching videos on YouTube, or going out and observing orchestra teachers work with their classes. Do whatever you need to do to develop a higher comfort level working with your students.

When you decided to become a band director, you probably made that decision because you had a passion for band and band music and wanted to share that passion with others. If you suddenly find yourself having to teach strings, fear, not passion, may come to the forefront. In order to be an effective orchestra teacher you will first need to overcome the fear factor. To do this, you should look at how similar the two jobs may be. The obvious starting point is that you will be giving students an opportunity to express themselves through music. Band students do this with wind and percussion instruments, and orchestra students do this with string instruments. If you're teaching a full orchestra it will have wind and percussion instruments also. Reading a score, explaining musical styles, developing good intonation, getting good attacks and releases, and counting rhythms are common to band and orchestra. Work from the familiar to the unfamiliar in order to be comfortable. The more comfortable you are, the less difficult the transition will be. Though most colleges and universities prepare students to be a band director or an orchestra director, few develop students to do both. This means that beyond receiving a cursory overview of string teaching or string playing, most students graduate without ever conducting both band and orchestra. There are more band teaching positions nationally in the United States than there are combined orchestra and band positions.

How Do I Start?

So, how do you get started teaching orchestra? First, you get as much training as possible before standing in front of an orchestra. That training needs to be hands-on with a string teacher/orchestra director. One of the biggest differences between band and orchestra is terminology. You must learn how to communicate with your students through the use of orchestra terms. Telling students how to use a bow has to start with you knowing proper ways to hold a bow. Before you can discuss bow placement on the string, you have to teach students proper ways to grip and control the bow. Identifying bow parts such as the "frog" (bottom part of the bow), and the "tip" (top part of the bow) is vital for getting started (see figure 1.1).

When deciding how a note should be bowed, you will need to analyze the piece that will be played. Bowing determines the overall sound of the piece. Will notes be played with the full bow or half the bow, on the string or off the string? Should phrases be long and flowing or have segments that are detached? It's the teacher's responsibility to make these decisions and determine what string techniques should be used to effectively interpret the piece correctly.

I'm a Band Teacher, and Now I Have to Teach Orchestra? / 5

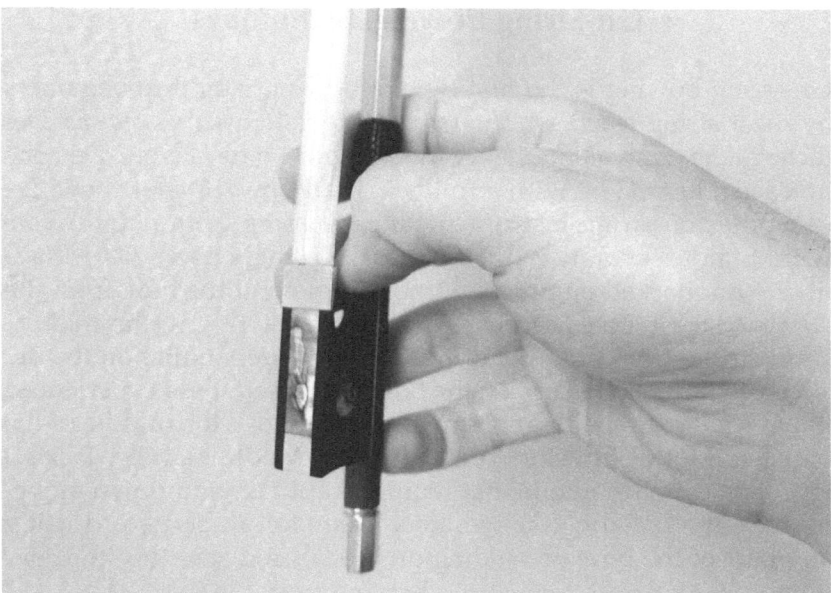

Figure 1.1.   Bow grip on the frog. Courtesy of Ben Scott.

The Importance of Using the Correct Bowing Terms to Describe How a Note Should Be Played

For wind players, there are five basic articulations: staccato (short and detached), tenuto (note played full value until the tonguing of the next note), marcato (an accented short detached note), tenuto accent or accent (emphasis placed on the beginning of a full valued note), and legato (a group of slurred notes). Articulation for wind players generally refers to attacking notes with the tongue in combination with air from the diaphragm.

For string players these attacks are done with the bow. There are more types of attacks for string instruments depending on bow placement and whether the attack is on or off the string. In order to get the desired sound, you must be able to tell your students exactly where to place the bow, how much pressure should be used on the string, if the bow is to bounce on the string, and which part of the bow should be used.

On-String Bowing Techniques

On-string bowing is the first type of bowing taught to beginners by most string teachers. The first stroke is known as *détaché*. Détaché is the equivalent of a tenuto note for wind players. Détaché notes can be played with a full bow, half bow, or short bow. *Legato* notes on string instruments means going from note to note without note separation (most times on a single bow). *Martelé* is a note with marked emphasis without removing the bow from the string. Martelé notes can be played from the frog to the middle, short stroke from the frog, or middle to tip depending on the desired amount of pressure on the bow to be used. Less-experienced players have difficulty applying pressure above the middle of the bow, so a lot of directors prefer frog to middle martelé. *Tremolo* is an on-string technique that requires rapid up and down movement of the bow on a single note. Tremolo can be played using any part of the bow depending on the desired sound of the conductor (see figure 1.2, on-string bowing from the frog).

There are other on-string techniques used by more experienced players. Most of these are variations on the techniques mentioned such as grand détaché, similar to a sforzando wind note, and martellato, a hammering of the note using the upper bow. Marcato and staccato are used referring to string playing, but the meaning of short and detached can refer to any of the short and separated notes bowing (martelé can be an on-string staccato or marcato note).

Off-the-String Bowing Techniques

There are some stylistic approaches that require off the string bowing. The most common of these is *spiccato*. Spiccato is a controlled bounce bowing. The notes are short and detached. Similar to spiccato is the *brush stroke*. Brush strokes are when the bow is lifted at the end of the note. The sound gives the listener the impression that the bow is brushing across the string (see figure 1.3).

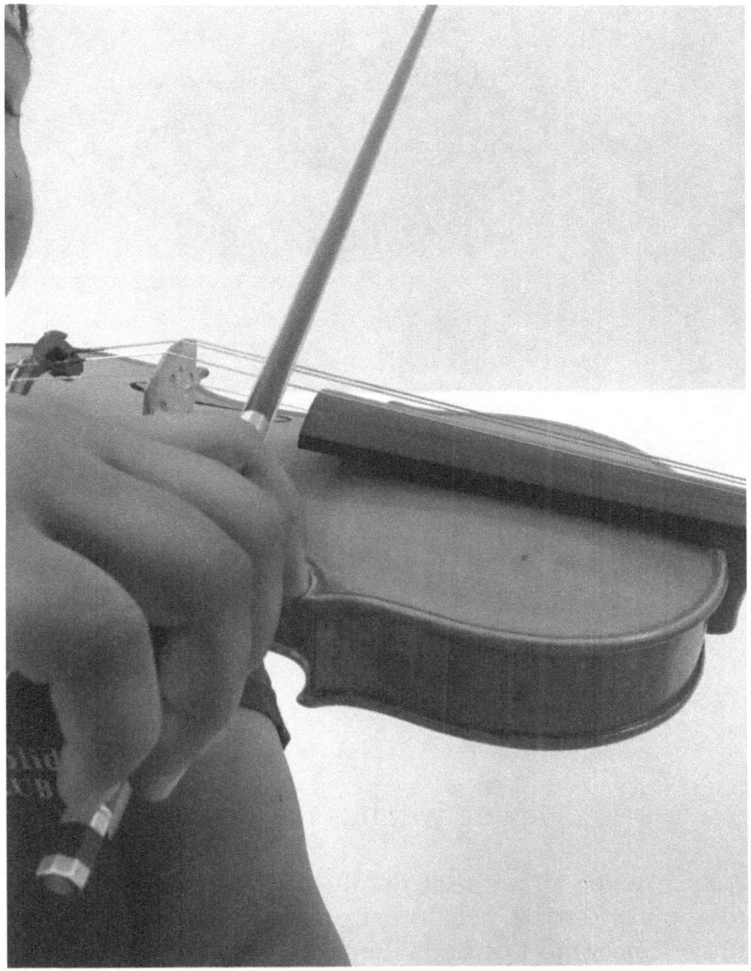

Figure 1.2. On-string bowing. Courtesy of Josalyn Walker.

8 / Chapter 1

Figure 1.3. Frog spiccato and middle-to-tip spiccato. Courtesy of Josalyn Walker.

Playing without the Bow

Pizzicato is a technique that involves plucking the string. Depending on the string instrument plucking the string can be using fingertips or the side of the finger. The space between strings determines how much of the finger will be used to pluck the string (see figure 1.4).

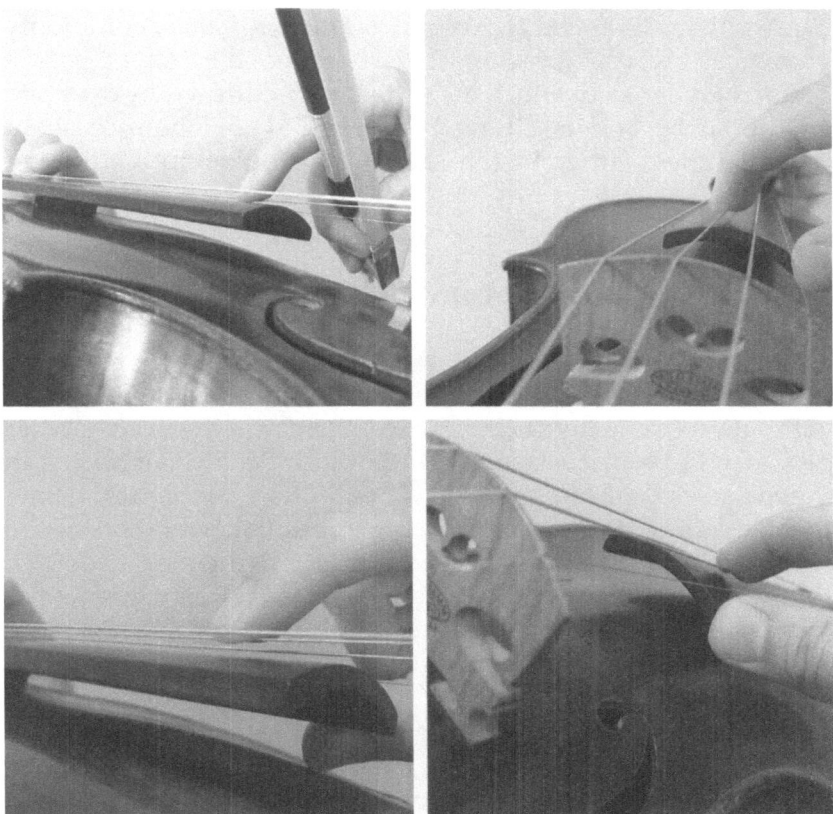

Figure 1.4. Pizzicato finger positions. Courtesy of Lauren Scott.

Playing Multiple Notes On the String or Off the String

There are variations of each of the strokes mentioned earlier that can be used for multiple note playing. *Jéte lent* (sometimes called flying spiccato) like regular spiccato is a bounce bow technique used to play a rapid succession of notes. This technique is used by advanced players and is generally found in more advanced music. Even though your full string orchestra or section may never encounter this style, you may have one or two advanced players who have it in a solo piece for auditions or competitions.

Another advanced technique is *saltato/saltando*, commonly known as ricochet bowing. This is when the player uses a bouncing bow stroke in which the bow is thrown or dropped on the string and is allowed to rebound and bounce again several times, either in the same direction or in a different direction.

Bow Pressure on the String

Though there are some bowings that want you to have a harsh sound, the preferred amount of pressure creates a smooth attack without any scratchy sound. This in combination with vibrato (which will be discussed in a little more detail later) helps to shape musical phrases. A short description of vibrato, sometimes referred to as "rocking," is a controlled vibration of the string done by compressing forward and expressing back out. Vibrato shapes the sound of a note by an even fluctuation of the sound wave. There are three types of vibrato: arm vibrato, wrist vibrato, and finger vibrato. Before we discuss vibrato in detail, let's talk about how to get a full sound from bow pressure.

Most string players are in agreement that the bow should not be applied to the string flat. The preferred way is to tilt the bow. Determining just how much pressure should be applied is a trial and error process. The "Goldilocks and the Three Bears" approach works. Not enough pressure will give a thin sound and too much pressure will yield a scratchy sound. Just enough pressure gives a clear single sound. If you hear overtones, the pressure is wrong. You also want to make sure the bow isn't too tight. Most violinists want a slight curve in the bow. If you hold the bow horizontal to the floor you should see the curve in the bow.

Vibrato on String Instruments

There are three types of vibrato for string instruments: wrist vibrato, arm vibrato, and finger vibrato. There are some violinists who feel that arm vibrato yields a beautiful round, full-bodied sound and wrist vibrato (sometimes called hand vibrato) yields a brighter, more brilliant, clear sound. Most young players start off learning arm vibrato because wrist vibrato requires more control. Arm vibrato is the "loosest" vibrato. This vibrato goes well with Romantic period compositions and slower moving block chords. Just like with arm vibrato, with wrist and finger vibrato the motion is the same. In all three cases the finger on the string is the same; contact should be made with the pad of the finger not the fingertip.

Young students will often stifle the sound by pressing the tip of the finger down tight. Players should apply just enough downward pressure to stop the string. Tightening up stops free movement. Encourage your students to have a soft touch. This is one of those cases where bringing in a violinist to demonstrate would be helpful. If there are no violinists available to come to your school, try a video chat app or go to YouTube, where there are several videos describing it. Be sure to screen the YouTube videos to be sure they are credible sources. The Online Violin Tutor on YouTube is a good place to start. You can also use #violinvibrato or #vibratoonviolin to search YouTube for more videos.

Violinists learn wrist vibrato by doing resistance exercises. One of the techniques used to develop wrist vibrato is to use the thumb and second finger to hold the violin and try to pull the violin away from the chin. Wrist vibrato is a moderately "tight" vibrato. Used in more open but still flowing passages, it's normally done with martelé bowing. The way the wrist bends is the natural position for vibrato. Each muscle needs to develop separately. A lot of teachers have students play D on the A string with their second finger and slowly use the resistance exercise motion. The motion should be carried out evenly so that the oscillations of the string will give a rich vibrating sound, thus the name vibrato.

Full arm vibrato involves use of the full arm. The performer pulls their arm back and forth on the violin but only slightly changes their finger's position, creating a change of tone. The thumb/second finger exercise and position are basically the same as wrist vibrato. Violin vibrato is when oscillation starts on or below a pitch. Some players start above the pitch slowly and increase the speed to add color and give a dramatic effect. This technique is generally used by soloists and not section players.

Finger vibrato is exactly what the name implies—vibrato done with the finger. Finger vibrato is the vibrato most used by section players. This vibrato yields a very "tight"-sounding vibration. Employed most commonly in fast-moving passages, it uses back and forth motions using one finger at a time. The string oscillates from below and above the pitch. Finger vibrato is generally used for higher notes and requires a little more control than full arm and wrist vibrato.

I'm not trying to teach you how to teach vibrato here; the intent is to make you aware that this is a way of refining your students' and your groups' sound. Cello and bass vibrato are different because of the size of the instruments and the way they are played, since both are placed on the floor. The basic concept of vibrato is the same, but the size of the neck and fingerboard make the grip and motion different. It is suggested that you use method books and guest artists or videos for the refinements needed to master the concept of vibrato for these instruments.

Chapter at a Glance

Preparing yourself for the new position should be your first priority. You want to know the basics and enough terminology to help your students have confidence in you as a teacher. Don't be afraid to bring in guest artists to help you and observe everything they say and do. Your students will respect you for making their progress a priority. They will know what you don't know and gain confidence in you as you continue to prepare yourself. If you can avoid trial and error, that would be good. Use instructional videos, a string teacher, or a colleague to help you gain an understanding of vibrato and other techniques. Honesty about your limitations will be your best course. As stated before, the students will know your weaknesses, and knowing that you are doing everything possible to do your best for them will build their confidence in you as a teacher. Once you get on the podium and begin to conduct, your band director skills and orchestra director skills will merge.

2

Building a String Program in Your School or Strengthening an Existing One

First Steps for Building a New String Program

As a band director, one of the most important things you probably learned about building a program was the importance of recruiting and identifying students you can bring into your program. The same is true for building a new string program. One of your first stops should be the guidance office. You will want to check the transcripts of the students in the lowest grade to determine who has had previous experience playing in orchestra at their former school. Then you should make personal contact with the students you've identified to invite them to be a part of your class.

One of the problems many directors have is forgetting the importance of personal contact. If you're a new teacher in a school, you're selling yourself as much as you're selling your program. Students won't separate you from the program in the program's early stages. You'll need to convince them why they need to be in your class. You should have a prepared response for the question, "Why should I take orchestra?" If you look as though you don't know why they should sign up for the class, they won't take the class. Your answer should be about how they will benefit from being part of a group of like-minded people.

What they can do for the program should not be stressed more than what the program can and will do for them.

If you're teaching more than one level of string classes, you will want to hear your new students and the current students play so that you can determine their playing level. If your school schedules students based on grade level, you may not be able to separate your students based on ability level. This may make choosing music more difficult, but it's not impossible to find music that won't bore advanced players or frustrate lower-level players. Later in this book, we'll address using chamber groups and smaller ensembles to challenge advanced players and help develop less-experienced players. In order to know where you want your program to go, you'll need to be clear on what you feel your mission is.

Developing Your Personal Philosophy of Music Education

Having a good personal philosophy of music education is very important. What do you want to impart on your students? How do you see yourself implementing your goals? How do you see music as a tool for student development? How do you view your mission as a music educator? Every child will not become a professional musician, but that doesn't mean they can't have a lifelong involvement with music. Students may become educated audience members, music patrons, or members of amateur orchestras but your mission is the same—help them develop a strong appreciation for orchestral music.

Some of your students may become administrators or decision-makers who will decide the fate of music in our schools. Here are some points that you need to make in describing your personal philosophy:

1. Explain how you see music as a lifelong pursuit. Every student won't become a professional musician, but all students will become consumers.

2. Share how music shaped your development. Include how you see music as an important part of the American education system.
3. Have a complete definition and description of music education in specific terms; avoid generalizing.

Once you have a clear, concise philosophy formulated, you're ready to share it with others. This means creating a support network that will help you get the needed resources to build a strong program.

Creating a Support Network

You can't build a strong string program in your school alone. You'll need to get all shareholders to buy into your vision (students, parents, administrators, community members, and school staff). In order to do that you must be very clear on how you want to see your program. Once again, be very specific and avoid meaningless statements that look good on paper.

After you've answered the questions mentioned earlier, you'll need to write your answers in a succinct statement. That statement should easily explain what you see as your personal mission. If you have a philosophy that speaks only to band you'll need to tweak it to include orchestra. Your personal philosophy of music education will be your contribution to developing a mission statement for each of your performing groups. Your syllabi and lesson plans will reflect the missions of your groups. You will need to create a resource network to help you implement your mission.

The National Association for Music Education has Music Standards that list what music education should do. Go to NAfME.org to view these standards. Use these standards to help you shape your personal philosophy, lesson plans, and the overall view of your program.

Your five-year plan will be the end product of everything being discussed here. In order for your program to survive for five years or more, you'll need help from the school district, your school administration, the school community, parents, current and former students, the faculty, and staff. During the first few weeks of school you should meet with each group separately to explain what you hope to achieve. Share with students how you see them aiding the program and what you see as the best way for them to support the program.

Most schools have a back-to-school meeting with parents in the first few weeks of school. This is your opportunity to meet with parents and give them an opportunity to help your program. Have a sign-up list of committees, trip chaperones, wardrobe consultants, fundraiser organizers, public relations, social activities, festival and performance helpers, and so forth. List all of the things that will release you to devote your time to teaching strings and building a program. Have a sign-up sheet there for a follow-up meeting to create an orchestra boosters group.

Meet with your principal and school business manager to find out the amount of funds you have available to develop a budget for music, supplies, and equipment. You'll need to provide school instruments for some students (cellos and basses especially). There are also funds available from some school districts to support string programs in schools. Talk to your music supervisor to find out what instruments the district provides for each school and the maintenance budget that's available for each school. String instruments generally cost more to maintain than most band instruments. Strings, bridges, and tuning pegs will be regular, ongoing expenses.

In order to attract and maintain students you will need the help and assistance from current students and former students (if there had been an orchestra in your school). Personal experience and recommendations from students will carry more weight than any other recruiting/maintaining campaign you may create. In the case that you need to reclaim students, positive one-on-one contact and testimonials will help immensely. Unlike other classes, students can choose electives, and they have a choice whether or not to stay. Knowing that you value their participation goes a long way toward keeping them and reclaiming them should they leave.

Planning for Your First Rehearsal

Writing lesson plans for your classes will be discussed later in the book, but now let's discuss practical planning. Practical planning is about preparing for chair placement and seating arrangements, instrumental storage, creating a welcoming atmosphere, music folders and music storage placement for easy retrieval—all of the things that will make the first rehearsal run smoothly. The way you expect things to go for the semester and year should be established during the first rehearsal. Classroom management and time management are very important. If students take too long getting their music, getting their instruments, and tuning their instruments, you'll have less rehearsal time.

During the first meeting with your students you should go over class procedures. Make it clear exactly how much time they will have to get their instruments, get their music, pre-tune, and get to their seats. Depending on the size of the group, all of those things can be done in five minutes or less.

As director it's up to you to model the expected behavior. Don't give them a timetable and then have them waiting for you to start class. You should be on the podium ready to start class at the end of the allotted time. You should be ready to take roll, tune the group, or start the warm-up if that's the beginning of your daily routine. You cannot expect them to respect your time if you don't respect theirs.

Once everyone is in place and ready to start, you should explain the expectations you have for the rehearsal. Example: "Okay, today we are going to concentrate on intonation and bowing for Brandenburg No. 3 rehearsal marks A through D." It helps to have the overall objective on the classroom board (electronic or manual). Your lesson plan will address exactly how you plan to achieve the objective. A typical rehearsal should have a warm-up, one or two rehearsal pieces, a sight-reading piece, or new piece of music.

Students should leave the rehearsal knowing exactly what they need to practice outside of class (for observers, this is homework). Do not over-plan or try to do so much that you can't achieve all or most of your goal. Have enough elasticity in your plan that should something not addressed in your plan come up, you'll be able to address it. Your students should leave class feeling as though they achieved something even if there's more to be done.

If students leave class feeling that the first rehearsal was productive they will look forward to coming back for the next rehearsal. The more organized you are, the better your rehearsals will be. The better your rehearsals are, the better your orchestra will be.

Chapter at a Glance

The most important thing you need to do as you start to build your orchestra is to have a clear understanding of what your function is. Having a personal philosophy of music education is the equivalent of having a road map or GPS system while driving—it gives you a clear direction for where you want to go. Everything you do to build your program will be an extension of your philosophy. Getting your students, their parents, and your administration to help develop a mission statement for the string program gives everyone ownership of the program. It's better to hear "our program" than "your program." People generally work harder on things they build than they do on things to which they don't feel an attachment. The most important thing to take away from this chapter is the importance of being organized and implementing your plans.

3

Creating a Syllabus and Orchestra Handbook

Before you meet with any of your classes you will need to create course descriptions and syllabi to clearly explain course expectations, class grading policies, class requirements, and basic class procedures. The class syllabus is a part of the orchestra handbook but because orchestra is a co-curricular group there are things that will be required for class credit that need to be clearly outlined. Some school districts provide syllabi for bands and orchestras and you can get a copy of that for your class. In case you need to write your own syllabus, this chapter will provide you with some details and suggestions you can customize to serve your purposes.

Grading Policies

For students taking orchestra for class credit, it is important that from the first day of class they are clear on what they are being graded on. Each item on which they will be graded needs to be given a percentage amount that will be added to achieve a one hundred percent total. The grading span for each letter grade must be given. For example, 100–95 = A, 94–89 = B, and so on. The lowest passing grade percentage should be made clear. Most schools have a uniform grading percentage scale that you can use for your class, and it should be in the syllabus. If performance participation is a class requirement, the syllabus should state how many performances a student can miss before failing the class. If homework/home practice is a percentage of the grade, that must be clearly explained and the percentage of the grade stated.

Some school districts prohibit extra credit or grade penalization for attendance so you may not be able to include class or performance attendance as a grading point. Since performances are the completion of class units, some school districts allow music teachers to use performances as unit tests. For grading purposes, you may wish to refer to performances as group playing assessments. Recording your performances to be used for guided listening evaluations by you and your students will support your assessment description. Once again, your music supervisor should have that information available for you to see and customize for your syllabus.

Developing a Handbook for Your Orchestra

As a band director you may or may not have a handbook for your band. When developing a handbook there are some important items that need to be included. First and foremost, your handbook should include your mission statement, a description of your orchestra program, concert attire, any fees required, assessment and festival information, planned trip information, and a personal statement from you as director stating your philosophy of music education and program expectations. This book should be a reference book for your students and their parents.

Since orchestra is curricular and co-curricular, it's important that the handbook includes a list of expectations for students who are not taking orchestra for class credit. This includes how many rehearsals a student can miss before being excluded from a performance or group trip. Students not taking the class for credit need to see what requirements they need to fulfill to be eligible for awards and trips. Listing these requirements will help to keep students taking the class for credit from feeling that students who are not don't have to follow the same rules they have to follow.

If you have fees and expenses associated with participating in orchestra, those costs need to be stated in the handbook, as do justifications for the requirement of those costs. If the school is not furnishing students with instruments, a list of vendors that students can buy or rent from should be included. If possible, purchase or rental prices should be provided for parents to see what expenses are associated with owning or renting an instrument. Because private instruction is an important part of student development, a list of private instructors and their rates should be included.

Once again, this handbook should be a quick reference with the complete description of the requirements, expectations, and financial costs associated with orchestra participation for parents and students to see. As is the case with developing syllabi, a lot of school districts have rules for orchestra participation. Those rules should be included in the handbook. A copy of a medical and health form that will be used for the year should be included to be removed from the handbook to be returned to you and kept on file.

A table of contents at the front of the handbook will help parents and students find specific information easily. Parents should not have to read the entire handbook to locate a specific topic (even though you want them to read the entire book). Your school administration should receive and review your handbook before you distribute it to parents and students. This will ensure that your handbook is in compliance with your school and school district's requirements.

You should also check with other orchestra directors and your music supervisor to make sure that your handbook covers all requirements and expectations that will help the orchestra program to be in compliance and be successful. If you have an orchestra website, it is helpful to post a copy of the handbook on it. Parents don't always receive handouts to be taken home, and posting it assures that parents can access the information easily and they will always know where a copy is.

Program Description

The program description should be stated clearly and unambiguously to make it clear what your program will be. Your vision of the program and what you expect your program to become under your leadership should be stated plainly. It is helpful to allow your students and parents space to help develop or amend the group's mission statement. This helps all stakeholders to buy into the goals and mission of the program. Instead of students and parents thinking of orchestra as "your" program, helping to develop the mission statement helps to make it "our" program. Ownership of the program will lead to their having accountability in the success or failure of the program based on a mutual vision. The program description is as important as the mission statement.

A Sample Orchestra Handbook

The following is a sample handbook for orchestra that can be adapted for your use. You should customize it to meet your needs.

Table of Contents

This is where you provide quick reference information for users.

Mission Statement

This should be a succinct statement of what the orchestra program in your school will be. You want to make it clear that the program will meet the needs of all students and will reflect the diversity of the community and will serve the needs of all students irrespective of race, socioeconomic status, cultural differences, disability, and gender identities. Students, parents, and you should have input into this statement.

General Handbook Description

This is where you include all of the information mentioned previously. It should include a brief welcome statement for new students and a statement of the importance of having returning students.

A Calendar of Events

In this section you should include all of the calendar dates that are required for grades and/or awards. Concert dates, assessment dates, trip dates, and any other required performances should be listed. You should also include which dates have mandatory participation and what dates can be excused without penalization (grade or awards points).

Concert Attire

A simple act that unifies a group is having everyone dressed in a uniform fashion. The handbook should outline the dress requirements and any costs involved. If the school is going to provide the attire, you need to outline the students' requirements for cleaning, maintenance, and repair or replacement costs. If the students are to purchase the attire you should include the vendor information and purchase costs. You should also state your expectations of appearance for performances (clean and well-kept attire). The important thing to remember is that uniformity in dress can lead to a mindset that leads to the achievement of a unified goal.

Fees

If there are fees that students have to pay out-of-pocket, they should be explained in this section of the handbook. This includes providing a schedule of when fees are due. It is very important that you itemize what the fees are for. If fundraising will be used to defray trip costs, a breakdown of percentages should be included.

Festival/Assessment Information

Most state music associations have a handbook that has a description of the importance of festival participation and a description of festival grades (I–V). These descriptions should be included in your handbook so that your students and parents understand the purpose and importance of festival/assessment participation. Most local, district, and state festivals are not competitions. Groups are graded based on standardized criteria. This provides you with a way of evaluating your orchestra's progress.

You may also wish to include your personal view of festival participation so that students and parents can understand why it's such an important part of your grading policy and why your students are required to participate.

Fundraising Overview

If fundraising will be used to defray students' out-of-pocket expenses, explain that clearly in this section. If you know the schedule of your fundraising activities those dates should be included in the calendar section of the handbook. You should be sure to check your school and school district's policies on fundraising before deciding on fundraisers or fundraiser dates. If the number and kinds of fundraisers will be determined by you and a committee of parents, explain how that process will work.

The National Association for Music Education has helpful information about forming and managing a boosters' group. Go to their website for information you wish to include about boosters.

Grading Policy

Your grading policy should be clearly stated. That includes the percentage of the grade each activity will receive. Class participation, festival participation, tests and assessments, concert and performance participation, special class projects, and other activities are a few of the items that should be included. Some districts have a grading policy that gives some percentages that can be customized for your use. Unfortunately, there are some parents and students who believe that participation in band or orchestra automatically guarantees a student an "A." Your handbook should make it clear that this is not the case for your class.

The handbook should be your go-to guide for how your program will operate. It will enable you to show students and parents that grades and awards are not given out arbitrarily.

Personal Statement and Philosophy of Music Education

This is where you as the teacher can make it clear why you became a music teacher and what your personal objective is. If you have not developed a philosophy of music education, you should visit the National Association for Music Education's website and look at their mission and goals statement and their strategic plan. You can write your philosophy based on your beliefs and this plan to ensure that your program has a solid foundation and is in line with other music professionals nationwide.

Everyone who reads your handbook should be able to get a complete understanding of what you want your orchestra program to be. "Back-to-School Night" is the perfect time to distribute the handbook and syllabi to parents. If you have not had time to involve parents and students in the writing of the mission statement, this is the time to ask for volunteers who would like to be part of its development. The rest of the handbook can be distributed and you can include a section that addresses the fact that the mission statement will be written by a group of stakeholders (parents, students, and you). The mission statement should remain the same every year, but each year you should include specific goals for the current year.

Chapter at a Glance

Once you've selected your students or they have selected you, it's important that they know what you expect of them and how they'll be graded. A good syllabus clearly states class expectations and your grading policy. Some of those expectations should outline how class participation, performance participation, playing exams, and other items unique to your program will be graded by percentages. Playing exams like those on SmartMusic (which is described in depth in chapter 10) can make grading your students and tracking their progress less difficult and less time-consuming for you. The syllabus will also be a go-to source of information for parents as it pertains to class expectations.

The syllabus is class-specific and there should be one for each class or course. A document that covers the general program and program policies is the student handbook. Because orchestra can be co-curricular there are expectations for graded and non-graded activities. If students are graded for performance participation, what are expectations for students who are not being graded? What happens if they don't come to performances? Participation expectations and rewards/consequences for all members have to be clearly spelled out. The syllabus outlines classroom expectations and the handbook outlines expectations for the performing organization.

A well-prepared handbook will make your program goals and expectations clear. Everyone who reads the handbook should know your music philosophy, your program's mission and what your plan to achieve excellence is. The handbook should be a snapshot of how you see your program and how important you feel music is to the development of the whole student. Along with general statements on how you want your program to develop, you should have specific goals and measurements for the achievement of those goals. New students and their parents should have a clear understanding of what you expect from program participants and what they should expect to receive as participants.

4

Writing Lesson Plans

Planning Lessons

One mistake made by a lot of orchestra directors is thinking that they don't need to write lesson plans. Lesson plans give you and your students a clear idea of what can and should be achieved during every rehearsal. The lesson plan should state clearly what the focus of your rehearsal will be, but also be flexible enough to allow you to address issues that may come up during the rehearsal. For instance, if your lesson plan is on proper bowing but you discover intonation problems, your plan should not restrict you from addressing intonation.

Working on the intonation problems has to be addressed and can be incorporated into the plan. If you're being observed by an administrator, it's important to explain the elasticity of your lesson plan for the day. Most school administrators are not aware of how orchestra classes or performance classes differ from other classes, so it's imperative that you make it clear when you can't stay "true" to the lesson plan and let problems go unresolved. Concert audiences may not be aware of your lesson plans, but they will be aware of whether or not you achieved your goals.

Before writing daily or weekly plans you should have a terminal objective for the semester. The terminal objective states your end point and your plans state how you plan to get to the end point. The objective should be broken down into units. Unit plans are broadly stated objectives and will include several specific goals. Each of these goals will be the basis for your weekly and daily plans.

Every part of your lesson needs to be reflected in your lesson plan. That includes the warm-up, rehearsal pieces, and closing exercises. If you say that you plan to work on attacks and releases, intonation or articulation, be specific on how you plan to address each issue during the rehearsal and state what exercises you plan to employ in order to achieve your goals. State in your plans how you will address issues you encounter with specific instruments or sections to fine tune things that class time will not allow (sectionals or individual coaching). Your daily or weekly plans should state a measurable relationship to your unit plan.

If your lesson plan is based on bowing for a specific section of a piece but your students are having technical problems, clear up the problems and return to your written plans. If you're being observed by an administrator, once again, it's important that you explain to them the elasticity of your lesson plan for the day. Each lesson should be building on a previous lesson and should have a measurable goal. Listeners may not be aware of your plan but they will be aware of whether or not your orchestra has achieved its goals. In music "close" is not good enough, it's either 100 percent correct or 100 percent incorrect.

Because each school district and state requires lesson plans to be stated in different ways, these sample lesson plans simply provide a guide for what should be included in your lesson plans.

Here Are Some Sample Lesson Plans

Sample Plan #1: Bowing

Bowing will be an ongoing issue with most young orchestras. It's important that you take time to explain the different bowing techniques and bow positions. One of the first steps is to identify the three parts of the bow that are indicated in music.

The bottom part of the bow is known as the "frog." The center of the bow is known as the "middle" and the top part is known as the "tip."

> Lesson: Today the class will rehearse Chorale #1, section A to section B using full down bows from frog to tip on the first half note and up bow tip to frog on the second half note. These bowings will be used in each measure throughout the entire section where there are half notes in the measure. When the first violins have quarter notes on beats three and four in measures five and six, the quarter note on beat three will be played from tip to middle and beat four will be played middle to frog. These bowings will be repeated throughout the section where there are half notes and half notes and quarter notes in the measure. To achieve bowing accuracy while playing, the class will play the Bach chorale on page 14 in the book of *16 Bach Chorales*: G. Schirmer Inc. The focus will be on listening to evenness in sound production of the full and half bows that are indicated. By the end of the lesson, students will demonstrate proper bowing with 100 percent accuracy.

Sample Plan #2: Intonation

Getting your orchestra to play in tune with themselves, their section, and the full orchestra should be a major and ongoing priority. Before you tune your orchestra each student should pre-tune their instrument. Having them tune to a tuner will be a good start but because you want them to develop their ear for good intonation you should have them tune to the concertmaster to fine tune. This serves two purposes: first, it helps the students develop the skill of cross listening for tuning purposes and second, it makes them aware of the need to make tuning adjustments as they play.

Using the Bach chorale from lesson #1, today's lesson will concentrate on the relationship between good bowing and sound production to effect good intonation (use the fine-tuning screws at the base of the strings to fine tune). As a warm-up for today's lesson the class will play a D-major scale two octaves on whole notes starting with a full down bow followed by a full up-bow.

Lesson: Today's warm-up exercise will be to play the D-major scale two octaves on whole note values with each note receiving a full bow stroke. Students will sing every other note in order to tune the pitches for ear development and accurate intonation. Once the students identify whether the pitches sound in tune, flat, or sharp the class will perform Chorale #1 from the *16 Bach Chorales* used in the previous lesson. Upon completing the chorale with satisfactory intonation accuracy we will move to our first rehearsal piece. The group will play our first piece, playing each note of section A as whole notes listening carefully so that we can achieve 100 percent accuracy on pitches (adjustments will be made when shorter note values appear). We will then play the music as written, concentrating on accurate bowing and pitch matching. The focus will be on listening from the bottom up matching the basses and celli for pitch accuracy and good intonation.

If it is possible, place a chromatic digital tuner near each instrument section so that students can visually see their pitch accuracy. There are several digital tuning apps that can be downloaded onto cell phones, making it possible for there to be tuners on every stand. After a few days using tuners during the rehearsal, have the students stop using them in order to become more reliant on their ears. Aural discrimination (using the ear) is the ultimate goal of this lesson. At the conclusion of each rehearsal piece the orchestra should retune. Pulling the strings while playing will cause the instruments to slip out of tune. You want your students to begin each piece with good tuning so that they can use their ears to fine tune.

Intonation will be an ongoing concern for your orchestra. Your students have to be made aware of how important playing in tune is. They will need to be able to play in tune throughout the entire range of their instrument.

Sample Plan #3: Tempo Control

One of the problems that can be prevented by proper bowing is tempo control. Most orchestras that rush do so because of inaccurate bowing. A measured, full bow from frog to tip will prevent rushing. For half bows, having an accurate bow placement for starting the bow is the key for avoiding short strokes and rushing. Showing students the importance of accurate bow starting position and bowing motion is very important from the beginning. Using the same Bach chorale you used in lessons one and two will help. As your students become more familiar with the rehearsal pieces the less difficult it will be for them to concentrate on the bowing, the intonation, and now tempo control.

Early on you may want to use an amplified "tick track" from a metronome to keep time so that you can walk through the orchestra to assist students with proper bowing. You can use a microphone to amplify a metronome through your speakers or use a Bluetooth-enabled system like a Megavox (Bluetooth amplifier) to allow the students to hear the beat (a lot of band directors have systems they use for marching band that can be used to amplify the metronome) (see figure 4.1).

> Lesson: Today's focus will be on tempo control. Building on the previous lessons, the class will concentrate on keeping a steady even beat through the use of measured bowing. We will concentrate on playing whole notes for four beats on one full bow. After the class has mastered playing controlled full bows for four beats we will repeat the process using half bows playing half notes for two beats. The final exercise will be playing quarter notes with full down bows and full up bows on one beat. The warm-up scale, D major, will be the scale used for each bowing exercise. Students will not use music to play the scale so that they can use their aural abilities to listen for tempo, intonation, and note accuracy. After these warm-up exercises, the class will use the Bach chorale used in the two previous lessons to work on tempo control. The first time through the music the class will use a "tick track." After achieving tempo accuracy playing along with the metronome, the class will play the chorale following the tempo with the conductor directing each beat without the use of the metronome. Tempo control will be an ongoing focus of the group until the conductor is satisfied that the group is not fluctuating the tempo in any way.

Figure 4.1. Bow in frog position. Courtesy of Josalyn Walker.

Once you're secure that your students can bow with tempo accuracy with a consistent beat, you can use the warm-up scale or etude to drive home the importance of watching the conductor's baton. Instead of giving each note of the scale, chorale, or rehearsal piece fixed tempo values, have students match their tempo and bowing based on the movement of the baton. Use unpredictable baton movements to force the students to watch without being able to anticipate your motion.

At first, the students will have sloppy attacks and releases and their bowing will be off but the longer you force them to watch you the better they will get. You will never be able to control the tempo if your orchestra is not following your conducting. You can make it a game of last person standing by eliminating students who rush, bow incorrectly, or attack too soon or too late until there's only one person left—the last person standing. This helps make a tedious activity a fun exercise. Another fun exercise is to have everyone except the concertmaster close their eyes while you conduct. This is a subtle ear training exercise that will cause the students to focus in on the concertmaster's sound.

Sometimes rushing occurs when students listen to those who are sitting near them who have a tendency to rush. A fun but very helpful way to combat that is to have the students sit somewhere else or have first violin players sit beside second violin players or viola players (scramble or scatter seating). Rushing only happens when students are able to gain momentum. Sitting in a different place or beside someone who is playing a different part fights against the rushing momentum.

This is also a subtle way to help develop cross-listening skills. When students return to their normal seating they will subconsciously listen for the parts they heard in the seating positions they were in during the exercise.

Sample Plan #4: Attacks and Releases

Another reason students rush and play out of tune is poor attacks and releases. Most directors don't think of attacks and releases causing bad intonation but if the fingers aren't set for an accurate attack, chances are the note will be played flat or sharp. Changes in finger placement will negatively affect pitch but the most recognizable problem with poor attacks and releases is rushing. If students are late on an attack they may rush on the attack. If they don't release in time they will rush to catch up. Stress the importance of attacks coming along with the conductor's motion. That's why the exercise from the previous lesson is so important.

Orchestras that follow the baton tend not to attack early or release late. The whole note/full bow exercise is very important. The whole note can't be released until the beginning of the next note if it is to be held for four complete beats. Cheating a note's value will lead to rushing.

> Lesson: In order to achieve 100 percent accuracy with attacks and releases students will start the note (attack) with the frog of the bow on the string and stop the note (release) at the tip by lifting the bow from the string or stopping the bow on the string after counting four full beats and counting beat one of the next measure in 4/4 time. Students will watch the conductor for the start and release of the note. We will use the D-major scale and alternate down bows and up bows on each whole note of the scale. At the end of the scale students will lift their bows off the string at the completion of the final whole note on beat one of the next measure which will be a whole rest. The exercise will be repeated until the group achieves 100 percent accuracy or the conductor decides that the lesson has been satisfactorily completed.

Chapter at a Glance

Good planning is the most important part of classroom management. Most disciplinary problems occur because of poor or no planning. Students need structured instruction and clear class expectations. Lesson plans give a clear direction for class lessons and instruction. They're like a GPS for where the lesson is going and what the final destination is. You won't get to the final destination in one lesson, but the lesson plan plots a steady course toward that final destination. The plans should state clearly what you want to achieve and how you will go about achieving it.

5

Creating a Parent Group and Support System

Developing a Support System for Your Orchestra

If you're developing an orchestra program in a school where you have a band program, chances are you have a band parent support group in place. All you will need to do for your orchestra is customize your current support system to include orchestra parents or develop a separate group. In some cases, an instrumental parent support group will suffice as long as it meets the needs of band and orchestra students.

This chapter offers some practical advice on developing an orchestra parent group that can stand alone or be incorporated into an existing parent group. The National Association for Music Education (NAfME) has a *Music Booster Manual* that outlines its policies on music boosters' and music teachers' responsibilities.

Establishing a New Parent Group

The most important first step in developing a parent support group is deciding on the group's purpose and how it will function. Will the group be a pool for chaperones or be a solid base for fundraising and other activities? Deciding this will determine what kind of leadership team you will have in place and how much oversight will be required of you. You don't want your parent group to go out on their own and do things that will not positively affect your program.

One of the first steps in forming the group is to establish the leadership structure. The smaller the leadership group the more effective it will be. Each member of the leadership team should have a specific function and purpose. You will need a chairperson who will coordinate all activities of the parent group along with you. This individual should be someone who can influence others into action, knows the community and your program goals, knows how to organize projects, and works well with others. It should be clear that the parent group cannot do anything without your approval and that their function is to assist you in furthering the advancement of orchestral activities in your school. Since you will have a mission statement in place and your philosophy of music education is clearly stated, all activities of the boosters' group should support the mission.

The next member of the leadership team should be the financial officer. This person is responsible for keeping a record of all funds brought in to the program and maintaining an accurate account of all expenditures. They will be the liaison between you, the school administration, and the school district (later in the book, you will learn about management programs and software that helps with this will be discussed).

The financial officer should be someone who can keep accurate records and can be bonded if that's a requirement of your school district. It is your responsibility to explain to the financial officer the school's policies governing fundraising, budget development, and purchase requirements (bid lists, etc.). They should not be the only person who can sign checks or have access to funds. Your signature should be required along with one other person on checks. This ensures that no expenditure can be made without your approval.

The booster group should not be responsible for purchases that are the responsibility of the school or school district. Every school has a business manager or financial secretary who handles all school purchases, purchase orders, and requisitions.

Once the boosters' financial person is selected, the two of you should meet with the business manager or financial secretary and/or principal to go over all of the school's and school district's financial policies.

The third member of the leadership team should be the activity coordinator. This person is responsible for overseeing all of the committees you'll need. There will be fundraising activities, travel activities, chaperone needs, uniform/wardrobe maintenance/purchase, and so forth. Various members of the booster group will be in charge of these activities and will have others working with them. The activity coordinator will help to make sure your "people resources" are not spread too thin. They will also make sure that two or more committees can work together.

Leadership Function

Once your three leaders have been put in place, you will need to decide on exactly what support you will need. The problem some directors have with forming a support group is not clearly defining needs, roles, and responsibilities. These roles and responsibilities should be outlined and be assigned to specific people and/or committees. These individuals and committees should have specific guidelines and must be able to work closely with you as orchestra director. As the director, you will have many responsibilities, and the boosters group should not create extra work for you.

Ideally, this group and its committees should be in place to assist you in developing a successful orchestra program. You should not micromanage: take advantage of the expertise of those you have selected and those who volunteer for committees.

The establishment of rules and guidelines (bylaws) is important. These rules and bylaws should clearly state the purpose and function of the group and the administrative limitations. It's imperative that the group knows that it must abide by school and district policies and cannot make decisions concerning your ensemble without your approval.

The following is a sample of booster group bylaws:

The _____ Orchestra Boosters Organization is established to offer support to the _____ orchestra. The function of the group is to provide financial and emotional support, chaperones, support activities, awards and recognition, and other tasks requested by the orchestra director. A checking account will be established and two signatures will be required to conduct any business or write/endorse any checks. One of those signatures must always be the orchestra director's. No business or official meetings may be held without the orchestra director's knowledge or presence. This does not include committee meetings as directed by the director or Orchestra Boosters Organization.

These bylaws should be consistent with your school's policies and must be approved by your school's administration. Since as band director you may have an existing band boosters group, you can also make it an instrumental boosters group and have committees specific to band or orchestra needs. If it is a joint group, take into consideration the different financial needs and account setup. Have each group keep accurate records of all funds. If your groups take trips together, there should be a combined bank account for trip payments and fundraisers. The band and orchestra committees should keep accurate records of all funds that are specific for band or orchestra.

It is recommended that two separate accounts be maintained and that you have a special "trip" (travel) account for each group. This is especially important if students will benefit from funds they raise during fundraising activities. Trip accounting is best done by maintaining records for individual students. This way when trip payments are tallied, you can figure in any percentages from fundraising that are credited to individual students using spreadsheets.

Some parents don't like students other than their own benefiting from their hard work. It helps that at the beginning of each fundraiser it's clear what percentage of the fundraiser benefits the group as a whole and how much will benefit individual students. You can include a statement to that effect in your bylaws.

Forming Committees

Most school districts have a Back-to-School Night or a first of the year Parents/Teachers meeting. This will be your first time meeting your students' parents. When you meet with the parents, it's good to have an agenda to outline what you and your group hope to achieve. Your music education philosophy, a proposed mission statement, your handbook, and a syllabus will help to make it clear what you hope to achieve. Having an agenda speaks to your organizational skills and that you value the parents' time.

At this meeting, have parents fill out cards with their name and contact information (name, e-mail, phone numbers, and address). You should also have a list of your expected needs so that they can select activities they can assist you with (match the parents' skill inventory with your needs list).

If you know fundraising activities you plan to have you can be specific, if not, you can ask for parents to sign up for a general fundraising committee. You will need chaperones for local and out-of-town trips, uniforms or special attire purchases/maintenance, equipment purchases and maintenance, and so on. This will be your first chance to organize your boosters—make the most of it.

Another important group formed at the beginning of building your program will be a publicity/social media committee. Publicity directly affects recruiting and helps keep your program from being one of the best-kept secrets of your school. If you or your students have accomplished something that deserves wider recognition, this committee should prepare and disseminate information on social media and to local news organizations. Posting pictures of performances, highlighting student achievements and successes, and announcing performances are also very important functions of a publicity committee.

As director, you'll have your hands full of music-related items, and making posters or posting on social media will take time away from performance preparation. You must be willing to "sell" your program and "advertising" is a very important part. Have your school's newspaper, web page, and all of its social media pages carry information about your program's successes and upcoming events. Have a parent or group of students specifically tasked with posting information about your group every week.

Chapter at a Glance

It's very important to have separate support groups for your band and orchestra as separate groups. Having a single support group for band and orchestra can have a negative effect on your orchestra. Because of marching band, pep band, and different band levels your orchestra students may feel left out without having their own group of supporters, both financially and emotionally. The costs of string equipment, repairs, transportation, and festival registrations are as important to the growth of your orchestra as they are for the band.

Organizing parents to assist you is very important to help show that you are as invested in the orchestra's success as you are to the success of the band. Orchestras have different needs from bands, ranging from equipment to music literature. If you're starting an orchestra from scratch you need to look at the cost of instrument purchases, equipment, repair and maintenance costs, workbooks, and music literature. Travel costs and festival registrations can be based on your band budget, but unless the two groups travel together the accounting has to be separate.

There is office management software that will be discussed later in the book that can be used to help organize and manage all of the tasks your boosters will undertake. The leadership team and you will be able to monitor these tasks on any Internet-enabled device.

6

Literature Selection and the First Rehearsal

Choosing literature for an orchestra involves several important components. First, you must evaluate the educational and instructional value of the music. The pieces selected should reflect the best periodic and stylistic qualities. If you select works of composers who are not from the major Western-music periods (Baroque, Classical, and Romantic), make sure your selections represent the highest qualities of music from those periods.

Second, selected music should have attainable performance levels and quality for your group. Your students and potential audiences should receive a pleasurable playing and listening experience. This doesn't mean you should pander to either group, but if your students don't enjoy the music they won't want to give their best efforts to perform it. If the audience, which will be made up of a majority of parents, can't enjoy the performance, they won't offer the encouragement your students will need to receive for your program to grow. The music should be engaging and interesting to both performers and listeners.

Third, the music should be challenging but attainable. You want your students to have to work hard to achieve a high-level performance but you don't want the music to be out of their reach. If they don't see themselves able to accomplish all that you expect of them, they may give up or become discouraged. Obviously, you don't want this to happen, because if you lose their interest it will be very difficult to get it back. You may have limited instrumentation (usually too few violas, cellos, and basses), so you may need to transpose viola parts for second violin players to play.

In order to preserve the integrity of the piece, your transposition should be done in such a way that the substitutions sound musically logical (don't write bass parts for violins). Should you have the scored instrumentation, your task is to make sure you maintain balance. Most developing orchestras have more violins than ideal so you'll need to make sure your group is not "top-heavy." This can be very challenging, and you should consider this when choosing performance literature for your group.

First Rehearsal

Music selection and rehearsal pacing are the two most important facets of the first rehearsal. The success of your first rehearsal will have a lasting impact on your program's growth and success. How your students feel at the end of the rehearsal will affect future rehearsals. Ideally, you want the rehearsal to end with your students eager to come back for the next rehearsal. Pacing is important because you don't want to skirt over problems or spend too much time on a problem causing your students to be bored.

Much care has to be taken to choose literature that will be challenging but not discouraging. In every group there will be students who are motivated and can play well. These students will master the music you choose. Conversely, there will be students who are less motivated and have less skill who will find it difficult to master the pieces you choose. Finding a happy medium between these two extremes is a challenge for you.

One way to challenge advanced players is to transcribe parts that are in the original score that may not be in the arrangement you're doing. You may be able to pair weaker players with advanced players as a team-building exercise. Before pairing the players make sure personalities and attitudes are compatible.

Students learn from each other during these pairings and the students helping other students tend to polish their skills as they teach.

During the rehearsal you will need to help students maintain their focus. Help them to identify the melodic line and use cross-listening skills to maintain proper balance and not drown out the melody. What you do in the first rehearsal should be transferable to every piece you will work on all year. Focus on teaching skills, not things that are not going to be used in future performances. This also points out the importance of selecting pieces for the semester or year that reinforce good orchestral playing.

Plan and chose your musical selections based on what you want to achieve and what you expect your orchestra to become. Whatever successes or problems you have in the first performance will be a direct result of your first rehearsal. Organization and planning will be the keys to your success.

Organizing the First Rehearsal and Classroom Management

Before your first downbeat in your first rehearsal, you should have some things in place. Students should know how much time they have to get their instruments and music and be seated. Once that amount of time has passed, you should be ready to begin your rehearsal. Unlike bands, orchestras have to tune four strings to be ready. Whether the group uses a tuner, your first chair violin player, or some other type of tuning mechanism, tuning should be controlled by you. Group tuning should be done after individual players have tuned their instruments.

Start by tuning A first. That way all players can tune and fine-tune together. Next, tune the violins alone, followed by the violas, cellos, and basses separately. The final act should be to tune everyone at the same time. In the first few rehearsals this may be time-consuming, but the amount of time shortens each rehearsal once your students know the regimen.

Once the orchestra is tuned your first rehearsal selection should be a warm-up. The purpose of this first warm-up is to get the group to follow your baton and listen to one another. The warm-up should be a chorale or block chord exercise so that the students can watch you and concentrate on attacks and releases, bowing, intonation, and listening for balance. Many young orchestras will be "top heavy," having more violins than lower parts. It's important that you get students to listen from the bottom up for ideal balance.

The rehearsal should be divided into at least three parts—warm-up, rehearsal, and cool down. The rehearsal selections after the warm-up in the first rehearsal will map out where you're going. These pieces will represent what your first performance will be. How you teach the rehearsal pieces will give students your expectations and what being in your class will entail. This is when and how you will establish your standards and what the character of your orchestra will be.

It's very important when working with the first rehearsal pieces that your students understand the importance of bowing and pitch/note accuracy and intonation. As the conductor you must have a clear understanding of the pieces. You will need to give bowing directions that are consistent with the style and period of the literature. Are the notes supposed to be played full bow or half bow starting from the frog to the middle or from the middle to the tip. These positions affect the sound. Are short notes to be played on or off the string? (This is where knowing spiccato and martelé are important.)

Before your students play passages with these articulations, you have to give clear descriptions based on the style or period. Needless to say, you must be familiar with how these articulations are played in each period and how each sounds. During the rehearsal there are no "little things" that can be fixed later. Everything covered in the first rehearsal is a "big thing." If students think that being "close" is good enough, that's how they will approach future performances of the music. Striving for perfection is how you achieve excellence. You may not achieve perfection (no one does), but you can achieve excellence through performance accuracy.

Ending the First Rehearsal

The way you end the first rehearsal is as important as the way you began the rehearsal. There should be a clear description of how you expect students to be prepared for the next rehearsal (practice expectations) and what you will cover in the next rehearsal. The rehearsal should not end with the students not feeling as if something has been accomplished. A statement like, "today was a good start, but there are a few things we need to clean up," will give positive reinforcement but also establish expectations. This leads into what's expected in future rehearsals. It also points out the importance of having a unit plan comprised of daily lesson plans.

Each daily lesson plan should take you to your terminal objective—a successful final performance. The lesson should conclude with students having a sense of accomplishment but also an awareness that there is more to be done. You should record the first rehearsal so that you can have a guided listening exercise with your students and so that they can hear what you hear. Recording the group will also give you an archive of recordings that document your group's growth.

Suggested Composers

The following is a list of the most recommended composers and arrangers of music for string orchestras. The list is compiled from suggestions from current string orchestra teachers.

Shirl Jae Atwell
Brian Balmages
Lauren Bernofsky
Elliot Del Borgo
Don Brubaker
John Caponegro
Sandra Dackow
Doris Gazda
Carrie Lane Gruselle

William Hofeldt
Lauren Keiser
Richard Meyer
Brendan McBrien
Robert McCashin
Deborah Baker Monday
Kurt Mosier
Soon Hee Newbold
Sean O'Loughlin
Todd Parrish
Bob Phillips
Steven Rosenhaus
Robert Seiving
Alan Lee Silvia
Robert Smith
Doug Spata
Richard Stephan
Douglas Wagner
Mark Jarrod Williams

Suggested String Methods and Publishers

The following is a list of string methods used by the author and recommended by orchestra directors and string teachers:

Strictly Strings Books 1 & 2—Jacquelyn Dillon, James Kjeiland, & John O'Reilly—Alfred Music Publishing
String Basics Books 1, 2 & 3—Terry Shade & Jeremy Woolstenhulme—Neil A. Kjos Music Company
Workbook for Strings Books 1 & 2—Forest Etling—Alfred Music Publishing
Essential Elements for Strings Books 1 & 2—Michael Allen, Robert Gillespie, & Pamela Tellejohn Hayes—Hal Leonard Corporation

Literature Selection and the First Rehearsal / 47

Foundations for Strings—Elliot Del Borgo—C. Alan/McClaren Productions

Note Reading for Strings—Eugenia Goldman—Soundwave Music

String Training Books 1 & 2—Kathryn Griesinger—Wingert-Jones Publications

The Sight Reading Book for String Orchestra—Jerry West—Wingert-Jones Publications

Essential Musicianship for Strings—Bob Gillespie, Pamela Tellejohn-Hayes, & Michael Allen—Hal Leonard Corporation

Muller Rusch Volumes 1–5—Frederick Muller/ed. Rusch—Neil Kjos Music Company

Developing Virtuosity Books 1 & 2—Lynne Latham, Thom Sharp, & Gayley Hautzenroeder—Latham Music Ltd.

All for Strings—Gerald Anderston & Robert Frost—Neil Kjos Music Company

Essential Technique for Strings—Michael Allen, Robert Gillespie, & Pamela Tellejohn Hayes—Hal Leonard Corporation

Artistry in Strings Books 1 & 2—Robert Frost & Gerald Fischbach—Neil Kjos Music Company

Applebaum String Method Volumes 1–3—Applebaum—Alfred Music Publishing

Measures for Success for String Orchestra No. 1—Gail V. Barnes, Brian Balmages, Carrie Lane Gruselle, & Michael Trowbridge—FJH Music Company Inc.

Advanced Technique for Strings—Michael Allen, Robert Gillespie, & Pamela Tellejohn Hayes—Hal Leonard Corporation

Suggested Literature for Orchestra

Table 6.1 is a list of selections compiled for the California Music Educators Association by Scott Krijnen. Music grades one through five are included here.

Table 6.1.

Last	First	Title	Grade Level
Clark	Larry	Antagonist	1
Newbold	Soon Hee	Appalachian Hymn	1
Williams	Mark	Fiddles on Fire	1
Newbold	Soon Hee	Russian Music Box	1
Meyer	Richard	Sahara Crossing	1
Balmages	Brian	Tribal Dance	1
Bush	Becky Phillips	Arctic Crossing	1.5
Balmages	Brian	Burst	1.5
Day	Susan H.	Cliffs of Moher	1.5
Meyer	Richard	Dragonhunter	1.5
Nunez	Carold	Little Symphony	1.5
Del Borgo	Elliot	Rite of Stonehenge	1.5
Strommen	Carl	Stone Mountain Stomp	1.5
Newbold	Soon Hee	Storm	1.5
Silva	Alan Lee	Storm the Gates	1.5
Balmages	Brian	Velocity	1.5
Newbold	Soon Hee	Viking	1.5
Monday	Deborah Baker	Beyond the Thunder	2
Gruselle	Carrie Lane	Boogie-Man Blues	1.5
Monday	Deborah Baker	Conquistador	2
Balmages	Brian	Creatures	2
Williams	Mark	Dramatic Essay	2
Brubaker	Don	El Toro	2
Giebler	Cyndee	Elasticity	2
Clark	Larry	Fable	2
Day	Susan H.	Flight	2
Spata	Doug	Gauntlet	2
Spata	Doug	Harrowland	2
Shaffer	David	Impravada	2
Calhoun	Bill	In a Quiet Place	2
Balmages	Brian	March of the Shadows	2
Longfield	Robert	Momentum	2
Yarmada	Keiki	Mystic Fawn	2
Meyer	Richard	Nightshift	2
Williams	Mark	North County Legend	2
Clark	Larry	Quintus	2
Sharp	Thom	Shadows in the House	2
Williams	Mark	Two Modal Sketches	2
Longfield	Robert	Vortex	2
Greissinger	Kathryn	Windchaser	2
Del Borgo	Elliot	Ancient Rituals	2.5
Parrish	Todd	Boreas	2.5
Turner	Matt	Chicken Foot Transplant	2.5
Lipton	Bob	Coiled	2.5

Last	First	Title	Grade Level
Greissinger	Kathryn	Echelon	2.5
Fishburn	Kathy	Espana Cani	2.5
Balmages	Brian	Intrada	2.5
Atwell	Shirl Jae	Kinetic	2.5
Barker	Paul	Momentum	2.5
Newbold	Soon Hee	Mythos	2.5
Curnow	James	Sagebrush	2.5
Balmages	Brian	Spartacus	2.5
Turner	Matt	Spy vs. Spy	2.5
Buckley	Robert	Stargazer	2.5
Turner	Matt	Tango Espressivo	2.5
Compello	Joseph	Tango Mariana	2.5
Nishimura	Yukiko	The Ancient Flower	2.5
Nishimura	Yukiko	Winter Milky Way	2.5
Rachmaninoff/ Longfield	Sergei	Adagio	3
Vivaldi arr. Frackenpohl	Antonio	Allegro in D	3
Mosier	Kirt	Blue Rhythmico	3
Meyer	Richard	Carpe Diem	3
Spata	Doug	City of Steel	3
Freese	Francis	Contrast in e minor	3
Bishop	Jeffrey	Declarations	3
Lipton	Bob	El Gaucho	3
Silva	Alan Lee	Escape from the Lost City	3
Silva	Alan Lee	Evil Eye and the Hideous Heart	3
Stephan	Richard	Fanfare and Frippery	3
Turner	Matt	Funky, Funky, Funky	3
Freese	Francis	Jazz Waltz	3
Nunez	Carold	M to the 3rd Power	3
Meyer	Richard	Mantras	3
Sharp	Thom	May, Maybe Not	3
Atwell	Shirl Jae	Modus à 4	3
Meyer	Richard	Momentum	3
Turner	Matt	Moonlight Odyssey	3
Holmes	Brian	Perpetuoso	3
Thompson	Chris	Phantom Watlz	3
Gruselle	Carrie Lane	Postcards From Russia	3
Silva	Alan Lee	Reels and Reverie	3
Gruselle	Carrie Lane	Scenes from the Emerald Isle	3
Tippette	Bruce	Surge	3
Monday	Deborah Baker	Synergy	3

(continued)

Table 6.1. *(Continued)*

Last	First	Title	Grade Level
Patterson	Andy	Te Dije	3
Lieberman	Julie	Terkisher Klezmerfest	3
Mosier	Kirt	Two Scenes from the Hollow	3
Mosier	Kirt	Waltz of the Wicked	3
Newbold	Soon Hee	Warrior Legacy	3
Safford	Alex	Blue Mountain	3.5
Ligon	Bert	Bossa Rojo	3.5
Ligon	Bert	Bossa Verde	3.5
Meyer	Richard	Cincopation	3.5
Meyer	Richard	Idylls of Pegasus	3.5
Ticheli	Franck	Rest	3.5
Safford	Alex	Revelation's Edge	3.5
Ligon	Bert	Road Trip to Rio	3.5
Barker	Paul	Titan X	3.5
Gardner	Robert	Today	3.5
Silva	Alan Lee	Adventures on Bainbridge Island	4
Spata	Doug	Argent Ege	4
Mosier	Kirt	Baltic Dance	4
Reiner	Andy	Blue Sky Basin	4
Trapkus	Paul	Conquest	4
Sharp	Thom	Dance for String Orchestra	4
Mosier	Kirt	Dance of the Iscariot	4
Atwell	Shirl Jae	Drifen	4
Meyer	Richard	Emerald Falcon	4
Newbold	Soon Hee	Firedance	4
Silva	Alan Lee	Forest Incantations	4
Newbold	Soon Hee	Iditarod	4
Meyer	Richard	Incantations	4
Silva	Alan Lee	Keystone	4
Meyer	Richard	Minotaur	4
Jenkins	Karl	Palladio	4
Sharp	Thom	Perfectly Natural	4
Mosier	Kirt	Red Rhythmico	4
Balmages	Brian	Rhythm Dances	4
Bishop	Jeffrey	Showdown	4
Laven	Steve	Snake River Stomp	4
Meyer	Richard	Vanishing Pointe	4
Warlock	Peter	Capriol Suite	4.5
Meyer	Richard	Elements	4.5
Whitacre	Eric	October	4.5
Britten	Benjamin	Simple Symphony	4.5
Seidenberg	Danny	Steel City Strut	4.5

Last	First	Title	Grade Level
Balmages	Brian	Urban Concerto	4.5
Hindemith	Paul	5 Pieces	5
Hindemith	Paul	8 Pieces	5
Barber	Samuel	Adagio for Strings	5
Mozart	Wolfgang	Divertimentos	5
Jarret	Jack	Elegy	5
Gershwin	George	Lullaby	5
Jarret	Jack	Meditation	5
Newbold	Soon Hee	Perseus	5
Nunez	Carold	Reflexions	5
Jarret	Jack	Romeo and Juliet	5
Wiren	Dag	Serenade for Strings	5
Safford	Alex	Stryes Rally	5

Chapter at a Glance

After all of the planning and preparation you've done to establish your new program, its success all comes down to the first rehearsal. The program can be well-stocked and everything can look good on paper, but the most important part of a performance class is how it performs. How you expect your group to sound, look, and prepare themselves comes down to the regimen you establish during the first rehearsal. Did you establish a terminal goal? For performance classes the terminal goal is the performance. No matter how good you look on paper, it all comes down to how you sound.

7

Having a Successful First Performance

The Importance of a Successful First Performance

As mentioned in the last chapter your first performance is one of the most important things for the building and life of your program. As important as the first rehearsal is, the first performance is even more important, because an audience will evaluate how well you and your students have done. Because of this, you will need to make sure your first performance is a true reflection of the standards you have established in your rehearsals.

Planning for a Successful First Performance

The success of your students' first performance will have long-term ramifications on the life of your program. The first performance will determine whether students remain in your program or will want to become a part of it. Word of mouth is the most important tool for recruiting and maintaining. If your first performance is good, your students will feel good about participating and encourage other students to join. Conversely, if your first performance is bad and your students don't feel good leaving the stage, the word of mouth will kill any momentum your program may have gained. After a good performance, your students will strive to recapture the joy of that first experience and measure their enjoyment based on the feeling they had at the conclusion of the first performance. As stated before, choosing the best literature for the first performance is one of the most important decisions you'll make. You want the literature to be challenging enough to hold your students' interests and cause them to strive for success but not be so challenging that they don't feel they can master it. Remember, your group will be made up of three kinds of students: highly proficient, proficient, and less than proficient. The strategies described in the chapter about choosing literature for the first rehearsal apply here. Obviously, most of the music you chose for the first rehearsal includes music that you plan to perform at some point during the year. Transcribing parts and simplifying parts may be required for a successful performance. This may mean simplifying parts for the less proficient or creating more challenging parts for the highly proficient. The success of your first performance may depend on how musical your transcriptions are. Be sure to keep the transcribed parts within the range of the scored parts. It's important that your students are always aware of the melodic line and how they need to make dynamic adjustments to make sure the line can be heard. Once students are aware of the importance of the melodic line(s), they will be more sensitive to adjusting the dynamics of the supporting parts.

When selecting music for the first performance there are several things you want your students to be able to do. Here are some of those things:

1. Play in tune with themselves and the rest of the orchestra
2. Listen across the orchestra to trace the melodic lines
3. Follow dynamic markings and expression markings accurately
4. Play with rhythmic accuracy
5. Use good tone and sound production through bow contact with the string
6. Play in the correct style using bowings that complement the period and style of the music
7. Use the complete range of dynamics

8. Play with good tone control and use note shadings
9. Balance within the section and through the entire orchestra
10. Develop good bowing

Once again, because every future performance will build on the success of your first performance, whatever problems or successes you have should be discussed during the next rehearsal. If you audio- or video-record the first performance, you should have a guided listening exercise the next time the orchestra rehearses to discuss next steps. How can you build from the positive things that you heard and/or how can you correct the problems identified? It's important that once you identify the problems that may have occurred, you immediately rehearse the skills needed to make sure your students correct them. Find a different piece that requires these skills, since you've rehearsed the performance music so much in preparation for the performance. You don't want your students' attention dulled by the music when you're addressing specific issues. Simply stated, start afresh unless you are going to perform the pieces again in the future.

First Performance Procedures

Because your first performance will possibly be the first time your orchestra has performed, there are non-musical things that need to be taught. Some of those things include going onto the stage, performance etiquette, carrying instruments as you walk onto the stage, concertmaster tuning on stage, folder uniformity, and of course, how to dress. The following addresses each of these items.

Stage Entrance and Seating

You want your orchestra to think and function as a single unit from the time it steps onto the stage until it steps off the stage.

That means you must explain, describe, and rehearse stage entrance and stage exit to your students. It's best that students go onto the stage in their section and seating order. Diagram the seating on the stage on the classroom board, identifying each student/part and how they should approach their seat/stand position. There should be one continuous stream of players going onto the stage, and when the last person from one section ends (such as first violins) the first person of the next section begins (second violins, violas, cellos, then basses, starting with the last stand first). Leaving the stage you should reverse the way you entered. Everyone should remain standing until the last person is on stage and is in position.

When leaving, everyone should stand at the same time and turn toward the exit. This simple act converts a group of students into an orchestra. Some orchestras stand when the conductor comes onto the stage. After the concertmaster tunes the orchestra, sometimes this individual will leave the stage and re-enter with the conductor. Students should be told how to hold their instruments and bows while on stage waiting for the conductor and between selections (called concert rest position). Some conductors like to have the orchestra lift their instruments and bows together before the initial downbeat. However you wish to customize your stage positions and procedures is up to you.

Performance Etiquette

Don't assume your students know what proper performance etiquette is. Remind them that there should be no talking or moving on stage prior to or during the performance. Gum-chewing should not be permitted. Students should be taught how to tap their heels lightly or their toes inside their shoes without lifting their foot off the floor. Foot-tapping is a distraction, but worse, it can cause rushing. Many recordings of school groups are ruined by foot-tapping picked up my microphones.

Establish the level of your students' stands so that they can look above the top of them to see the conductor. For uniformity, decide whether students will sit on the edge of their seats or sit with their backs on their chairs. This decision affects the uniformity in bowing, so it's not a petty decision. Performance etiquette impacts your overall performance, so plan everything carefully. After the first performance these items will be an automatic regimen.

Carrying Instruments Going on Stage and Leaving the Stage

The way your students carry their instruments onto the stage and off the stage is not just about the visuals, it's very practical. You don't want your students carrying their instruments in such a way that they can be bumped or hit. Bridges have been broken or knocked out of position by a simple bump or knock. Don't let your students carry their instruments in such a way that they can hit another student, stand, chair, or wall. Most directors have their students carry their instruments tucked carefully against their bodies in a way to protect strings, tuning pegs, and bridges. Cellos should not be carried to the side; they should be carried in front of the players. Protecting the bridge on cellos and basses is the most important part of carrying the instrument on and off the stage.

Concertmaster Tuning on Stage

Once everyone is on stage, the first official act of the concertmaster is to tune the orchestra. As discussed in the section on tuning and intonation, the violins should tune first. The tuning progression should go from the highest instruments to the lowest and then everyone should fine tune to "A" before the tuning is concluded. As long as one person needs to tune, the concertmaster should remain standing. If the concertmaster leaves the stage to re-enter with the conductor, she should remain standing until the final tuning has been completed. Once the concertmaster and conductor come onto the stage the conductor has the option of having the concertmaster play the tuning note one last time.

Folder Uniformity and Concert Attire

What may seem a simple act of having the same folder for their music, uniformity in having the same folder has the effect of having a group mindset (music stores often provide free folders for groups or charge a nominal fee). Visually there is nothing more distracting than having mismatched folders or torn folders going on stage. If possible, have separate folders for everyday use and for performances. Purchase leather-covered folders or use cardboard folders that are not frayed on the tops. Groups are judged by the way they look going on stage, and that first impression gives the audience a positive view of your group. It also makes your group feel more uniform.

Performance Attire

In your first year with your orchestra you may not have uniform concert attire, tuxedos or long dresses, but that doesn't mean the group can't dress uniformly. You may choose to have young ladies dress in black skirts or dress pants and white tops and young men wear black dress pants, white dress shirts and black bow ties or straight ties, and dress leather shoes (no sports shoes). Some schools have groups wear all black. It doesn't matter what you decide your group should wear, it's important that they wear the same style and color scheme.

You want your group to feel like a single unit rather than a ragtag group of individual players. Dressing uniformly helps the group mindset and leads to a "group mentality." This mentality leads to performing in a unified manner. The concert/performance attire should be explained in your student handbook. Eventually you will want to purchase dresses for your young ladies or have them made (some parents in your booster organization may have dressmaking skills). There are several companies that sell affordable tuxedos and formal long dresses. If you're going to require students to purchase their own outfits, they should be told in the beginning of the year. If you're going to purchase outfits with school funds you need to include the costs in your budget.

Remember, the purpose of uniformity in attire is that you are a unified force with a single goal—an outstanding musical performance. In the orchestra handbook you should explain clearly why it is important that your students dress uniformly. As mentioned earlier, it's more than just a visual effect; it's a mindset that says we are one, a group of individuals functioning as one unit working toward a common goal.

Chapter at a Glance

There are many components involved in developing a group mentality. You want your group to perform as a single unit. How they dress, how they carry their music and instruments, how they enter and exit the stage, and how they carry themselves on stage are very important in developing and maintaining a group mentality. If you video-record rehearsals and performances your students will immediately recognize this importance. At festivals/assessments judges almost always comment on stage entrances and stage decorum. Most assessment sheets have a category addressing those items. Concert audiences don't have formal assessment sheets but they do notice. The most important group that will notice is your orchestra. Sloppy stage entrances affect the way groups perform. The lack of discipline from stage decorum negatively impacts performances. You can't expect good audience decorum if they don't see it being modeled on stage.

8
Festival Preparation and Performance

Festival Performance Planning

Preparing for a festival or assessment is very much like preparing for your first performance, with a few obvious differences. First, by the time you start preparing for a festival/assessment, your group should have had one or two performances and be well rehearsed and prepared for adjudication. Second, unlike a concert, an assessment has three adjudicators listening to your performance and following a score to judge performance accuracy.

Festival Information and Description

Every state music association gives a description of the purpose of festivals and the importance of festival participation. In the description there's an explanation of festival grades. You should include the description and explanations in your orchestra handbook so that your students and their parents can understand the importance of the festival. Generally, these festivals are not competitive on the local and state levels. Groups can receive ratings (Superior, Excellent, Good, Fair, and Poor) or receive comments only.

During the performance the judges write and voice-record comments that describe the areas done well and those that need improvement. There is no winner or loser in these assessments. There are festivals on the national level that you can participate in that are competitive. The judges use the same criteria for judging but assign numeric values to each category. The numbers are tallied and first, second, or third place is awarded based on the top three highest scores.

You should also include your personal view of the importance of festival participation and why your students are required to participate. You will need to show the percentage of your students' grade that is associated with festival participation and that you expect 100 percent participation from your students. Your handbook should copy the explanation of ratings exactly as printed in the state association's festival handbook. To show the educational value of festivals you should make it clear that your orchestra's growth is not just determined by the final rating.

The adjudicators only see a snapshot of what your orchestra has done and judge based on a standard of performances they have witnessed or expected from personal experience. You and your group know how far along they've come and how well they performed based on their preparation. Only they and you know if the festival performance was as good as expected.

Preparing to Be Adjudicated

On paper, preparing for a concert and preparing for adjudication involve the same things: performing attacks and releases accurately, good intonation, good balance, rhythmic accuracy, and bowing accurately for good articulation and style accuracy. What is different is that the standards for performing for an audience of untrained listeners and performing for judges following the score is very different. An audience won't normally know the difference between martelé and spiccato since both are short and detached, but a group of trained judges will.

Score Study

How well you as the director prepare before adjudication will determine how effective you are. Score study enables you to plan out the best way to teach the festival pieces to your students. Work through how you will present and rehearse the pieces with your orchestra. Determine what sections of the pieces will be most challenging to your students and decide the best way you will present and rehearse these difficult and challenging parts. The more prepared and organized you are before the rehearsal, the more organized the rehearsal will be. If you come across parts that are beyond your scope of knowledge, seek out help or assistance.

Contact another orchestra director, former college instructor, or a private teacher or master musician if necessary. The bottom line is that if during your score study you discover your personal limitations, don't allow false pride to get in the way of you getting help.

Make Notes on the Score

Because the judges will have a score for each piece you'll be performing, you need to mark your scores so that you won't miss the challenging parts that they will see. Circle sections of the pieces that will need special attention. It may be that you need to give a cue or simply a reassuring look to help build confidence.

Whatever the case may be, you'll want to be prepared so that you can prepare your students in advance. Don't give the judges your work score as one of the copies they'll use, because it will provide them with a guide to recognize your problem areas or weaknesses. For teaching purposes, on your work score, write in the solutions you have for problem areas.

Teaching the Music for Adjudication

As you study the score you should make notes for yourself to use to teach the music. These notes are a step-by-step approach you'll use as a teaching plan for your lesson plans. The lesson plan will state what your goal is in general and these notes will be your complete description of the way you plan to achieve the goal and execute your plan. Unlike the lesson plan that's written for non-musicians to be able to follow, your teaching notes will be more detailed and use terminology musicians use in preparing for a performance.

One of the first and most important parts of teaching music for adjudication is that from the beginning, you must address everything in the score. You don't learn notes and rhythms first and come back and learn dynamics and expression; you learn everything first time through. If you sight read the pieces before you start the process of teaching them, it's okay not to stop for items being missed or overlooked; you'll be preparing your students for the skills they'll need for sight reading, which is an important part of the festival.

Sight reading without stopping will give you a chance to identify problem areas in the music that you may not have recognized as problems during your score study.

When you begin the process of teaching the music, you must choose your words carefully. You don't want to inadvertently create problems or cause your students to develop insecurities or fears of difficult parts. Frustration breeds frustration, so it's important that you don't allow any fears you may have to be transmitted to your group by your word choices. Always go from the familiar to the unfamiliar. Start with what your students know about the style, period, and different performance practices from similar pieces. This is why selecting music for the first rehearsal is so important.

If you choose music for the first rehearsal that is consistent with the skills required for good orchestral playing, you can expand on those skills for the adjudication pieces.

The following should be your "playbook" for preparing for a festival:

1. Be methodical. Make sure you don't select large chunks of the music to teach in each class period. Based on the level of difficulty and how meticulous you'll need to be, allot

Festival Preparation and Performance / 65

yourself enough time to give thorough explanations and for your students to put your explanations to use. Don't leave a section until the students have acquired the skills needed and have performed at a satisfactory level.

2. Locate sections in the piece you're working on that may appear in the music for different orchestra sections. If the first and second violins have the same material in different parts of the music, teach it to them both at the same time. If they have the same part but in different keys, teach them the rhythms, bowings, articulations, and other items that are the same. If you can teach multiple orchestra sections the same melodic lines or parts at the same time, you won't have to worry about students getting bored and having discipline problems (boredom is the main reason for discipline problems in orchestra).

3. Have students clap, pat, or sing challenging rhythms. Once again, in most of the music you choose, you'll find that melodies travel throughout the orchestra. During your score study you should've discovered this. Trace the melodies and counter-parts and bring them to the attention of your students. There will be students in each section who will be able to identify the similarities in their parts and the parts of other sections, so solicit their help in assisting their classmates. Have these students point to the section where they hear the melodic lines being played. After they do that, have only the sections that have the melody play. Without any other parts playing, have the students playing the melody match the dynamics of the section that played the melody before. Emphasize the point that it should sound like one continuous line with no measurable breaks. Next have the full orchestra play and adjust their dynamics in such a way that the melody can be heard. Compare the passing off of the melody with the passing of the baton in a relay race.

4. Use long tones to demonstrate the phrase shapes and dynamics. Before playing a two-measure or four-measure phrase, have the orchestra play a long tone the length of the phrase and follow the crescendo and decrescendo

markings (they may have to use down- and up-bow combinations to sustain one note). Be sure to emphasize that the diminuendo/decrescendo should start at a stronger level than it ends, not suddenly get soft. Too many groups play subito (sudden change) rather than a gradual change. Adjudicators know that this is a common problem for orchestras and when they hear an orchestra execute it properly they know it's something that has been discussed in class.

5. Follow period accurate articulations. Remember, short/detached notes are played differently in different periods. Be sure to indicate on string or off the string short notes and which part of the bow should be used. Some tenuto notes (full value notes) are played full bow or half bow. You and the concertmaster should go through the score together to decide on bowing for the entire piece. Once the violin bowing has been determined, you can go through the pieces with the principal viola, cello, and bass to decide their bowings. Bowing is a major part of a successful performance. Some pieces come with bowing indicated and others will require you to mark the parts. This is another case where you may need to consult someone who plays or watch a video of an orchestra performing the pieces to determine the best bowing. Some bowing is logical but some requires string playing knowledge to achieve accuracy in performance.

Once you have concluded the preceding steps, the orchestra can play through the piece section by section, following all markings. Pacing of the lesson is important because trying to rush through the piece to cover a lot in one rehearsal may mean overlooking important details. Working too slowly can cause your students to become bored and turned off to important details you're trying to bring to their attention. Many directors have difficulty determining the pace at which student learning should take place. There's no exact formula, because students will have varying abilities.

Deciding on when to press on with a lesson and when to pull up is difficult. You should gain a sense of your group and know when to step away from your quest for perfection.

One solution for pacing is deciding on how to break your lesson/rehearsal into manageable units. Trying to achieve too much too soon can be counterproductive. Students can be discouraged or overwhelmed if you try to do too much in one rehearsal. They may leave class thinking they have failed because they didn't achieve what they thought they should have. During your score study you should decide exactly what parts of the piece pose the greatest challenges. Aim for a reasonable amount of time to spend on specific sections of the piece.

During the rehearsal, be willing to scale down on the lesson. Try to recognize the body language and facial expressions of your students to know when it's time to move on. This doesn't mean to leave something incomplete; it means that if you must spend more time to get something right you should leave the piece or work on something less demanding. Once again, keep a realistic sense of what you can accomplish.

Record Your Rehearsals

So that your students know what they need to work on, record your rehearsals. Sometimes students think you're just going over pieces they play well and don't try to make corrections. Record them and then do a guided listening exercise using the adjudication sheets the judges will use. Play the recording for them to comment on with no comments from you. Let them be the adjudicators. After they have made their comments, play the recording again and make your comments/observations.

Have the students read their comments on each adjudicated category (tone quality, balance, articulation, etc.). Encourage the students to not make their comments personal, but to refer to specific sections of the group and piece. For example: the first violins didn't play the diminuendo in measures four through eight effectively, or, the cellos need to increase their volume in section A for us to have a better balance. You may be surprised at how much your students will hear once they assume the position of adjudicator.

Immediately after listening to the recording, have the group play through the piece they critiqued and record it. Compare the two recordings and then decide if they made enough of a difference in the second performance of the piece to obtain a higher grade. In most cases, this exercise will make students more aware of what has to be done on a daily basis to achieve a successful festival/adjudication performance.

Chapter at a Glance

The most important part of preparing for a festival is getting your students to understand the purpose of adjudication. First and foremost, a festival is not a competition; the only group you're competing with is yourselves. What matters most is to achieve the best possible performance you can. Getting your students to take an active part in their preparation is the ultimate goal. Once they become active participants rather than passive participants, the educational value of the preparation increases. Judges only see a snapshot of what you've achieved but they are unaware of where you were. You and your students know what you overcame in order to perform the way you did.

Once you've gone through adjudication, you should have a guided listening exercise with the recording of your festival performance. Remember, everything musically you hope to achieve at festival should be introduced on day one, even if you aren't working on the actual festival music.

9

Program Maintenance

Maintaining Your Program

After you have started your program and established standards, you'll need to take steps to maintain and grow your program. Planning and setting goals are very important in this process. Your mission statement, philosophy of music, unit plans, and daily lesson plans are intricate parts of your program maintenance as well as program development. Good planning and management are vital parts of the process of maintaining your program. Students don't want to be in classes that they feel are a waste of their time. Positive word of mouth from students is a good recruiting tool and students who enjoy class activities tend to stay.

Developing a Five-Year Plan

Having a five-year plan is like having a GPS system for your program. For programs to be maintained, you'll need proper functioning equipment, a full library of music, good storage areas, and of course, students. As you set program goals, you need to make sure they're consistent with your philosophy of teaching. Your philosophy should state what you want to do as an educator. What do you want your orchestra to gain from working with you? What resources do you need to achieve your personal goals?

Your goals will guide what you want your students to achieve. Once you're clear on what you want to achieve as a professional, you can then decide what you want your program to achieve. Visualize the end product first and then plan how you want to achieve the finished product.

Your five-year plan should have specific goals and a timeline for completing those goals. The stronger the foundation, the stronger the finished product. The plan should involve teaching goals, basic management, and planning for equipment and instrument purchases. You should plan for recruitment, retention, and reclaiming. Even though you want to recruit well in the first two years, you want to devote most of your efforts to maintaining the students you have.

In the unfortunate case you lose students for whatever reason, you want to have a plan in place to reclaim any students you lose (though there may be some you don't want to reclaim). There are usually signs that students don't plan to remain in your program, and if you keep your fingers on the pulse of your group you can encourage those contemplating leaving to stay. Address those issues in your five-year plan. There are basically two reasons students leave a new program—boredom or being overwhelmed by difficult music.

Classroom management should not be one of the reasons students leave. Good planning on your part should avoid classroom management or disciplinary problems that turn students off.

Maintaining Equipment and Equipment Purchases

If there has been a program in your school before, you'll need to take an inventory of school-owned instruments and assess their condition. There are some obvious problems that can be seen easily and some you'll have to look for. Cracks, open seams, sound posts out of place, bridges out of line or off completely, and tuning pegs are the most common problems. Quick checks will help. Although these are easy to find, they are not always easy to fix, and most need to be repaired by a qualified repairperson.

- Cracks—Look over the instrument top to bottom, front and back, inside and out. Small cracks will get bigger over time if not fixed. Do not attempt to glue a crack. Special glues and vises are used to seal cracks and keep the instrument aligned properly.
- Seams—Cellos and basses tend to have seams separate because they're generally not stored in cases and are subject to room temperature changes. Less expensive instruments are more susceptible to seam separation. Get this repaired as soon as possible. It rarely happens to violins and violas because their cases offer protection.
- Sound posts—Sound posts will fall out of place if the instrument is dropped or bumped hard. You can look inside the instrument through the F hole and see if it's still in place. If it isn't, take the instrument to the repair shop. This problem is easy to see but it's not easy to fix.
- Tuning pegs—Tuning pegs will sometimes get stuck and sometimes not stay in. This is generally because of weather conditions. There are quick fixes for this problem but you'll still need to go to a repair person for a longer-lasting solution. If it's stuck, sometimes a tight grip and a twisting motion will get it loose. If you use any type of tool like pliers to untwist, cover the peg with a cloth to prevent scratches or other damages. If the peg won't stay in place, an easy fix is to wrap paper around the peg to get a tighter fit to hold it in place. Don't wrap adhesive tape around the peg. The adhesive will spread into the peg slot and cause stickiness. You will create a new problem fixing an old one (see the bridge position in figure 9.1).

During the first year of your program there will be purchases you have to make to help establish the program. As mentioned before, there will be very few students who own a bass or a

72 / Chapter 9

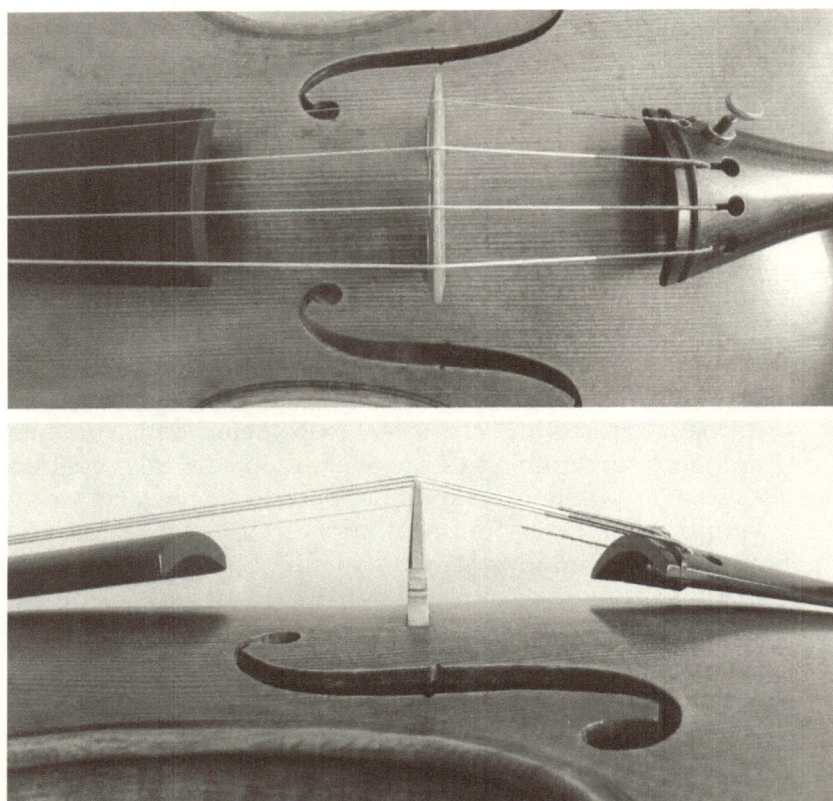

Figure 9.1.   Proper bridge position. Courtesy of Lauren Scott.

cello (transporting these instruments to and from school is also a major problem). In order to make sure your students can play these instruments in class you will need to purchase them for the school. Of course, if you purchase the instruments you will also need to purchase storage racks to hold them.

There will also be a need for storage cages or storage shelves to hold violins and violas. As you build your music library you will need file cabinets and storage bins for folders. Storage bins or shelves should be located near the rehearsal area so students can retrieve their music in a timely manner that doesn't delay the start of the rehearsal. In most cases, your band room will also double as your orchestra room. If this is the case, be sure to have separate storage areas for music and instruments for each group. This will give each group ownership of the room.

Program maintenance also includes maintaining your classroom. Keep chairs, stands, risers (if you have them), storage areas, and walls in good order. Wobbly stands or bad chairs are problems that affect student attention and focus. Like having school instruments in good working order, having equipment in good working order is vital. The orchestra is not rehearsing in the band room, they're rehearsing in the instrumental room or the orchestra room (which also happens to be the band room).

Remember, you're no longer the band director who has orchestra classes, you're the band and orchestra teacher/director. This may seem like something unimportant to you but it's important to the identity of your orchestra.

The Importance of Individual Recognition and Praise

One of the best ways to keep students in your program is to recognize individual or small-group achievements. There are many ways to do this, from posting on your group's social media pages, or school website, or posting pictures on school walls or in the orchestra room. Take a picture of the individual or group and post it as a student spotlight, player of the week, or section/ensemble of the week. The esteem of the recipient(s) will rise and other students will aspire to achieve such recognition. This will create the kind of environment in which players want to remain.

You can leave the pictures on a bulletin board or on the website all year. At the end of the year you can select a group or individual for a Section of the Year or Most Valuable Player Award. Students who are coming to the school or your program for the first time will notice that they can be recognized for their achievements and see that they will be valued in your program. This means so much for recruiting and retaining for your program. Recognition of excellence begets excellence.

Some schools still have printed newsletters that they send home with students. There should never be a week that passes that there's not something positive about your students and/or your program in it. The PTSA in most schools uses a listserv e-mail system to disseminate information about the school. Have the publicity committee of your parent group profile a student or ensemble each week. Remember, if students feel valued they will stay in your program and will be more apt to encourage other students to join.

The best way not to have to reclaim students is not to lose them in the first place. You should also send positive information about your program to the middle school and elementary school. Your five-year plan will include these students as future members, and if they see positive information about your program their interests will develop.

Don't just recognize students who have obvious accomplishments; that won't really help your program grow. You should have an award and recognition for students who contribute to your program but are not the most talented. These students who are in "supporting roles" can receive an "unsung hero" type of reward. The top players will always return to your program, but the players who work hard behind the scenes won't return unless they know their participation is appreciated. This may sound cliché, but you're a teacher first. It's your responsibility to reach every student and create a nurturing environment.

The more aware you are of the human dynamic involved, the more you will succeed. Recognition is equated with value, and the more you recognize your students the more valued they will feel.

Chapter at a Glance

Program maintenance starts the very first day of school. The kind of environment you create in your classroom, the planning you do for lessons, the library of music you choose, how you keep your students engaged, and your performance standards all determine how well maintained your program is. Developing a five-year or long-term plan will keep your focus on growth, quality, and quantity.

Your personal philosophy of music education and your program's mission statement are vital parts of your program maintenance. Organization is the key. Trying to build your program as needs arise is the formula for failure. You need to have a "road map" for your journey. Students won't want to stay in a program that doesn't seem to be headed in a positive direction. Using all of the support groups and strategies outlined in previous chapters will help you maintain a viable program.

Having a clean, welcoming environment and well-kept, functioning equipment is important. Instruments in poor condition or non-working order have a negative impact, consciously or unconsciously. Fix them or discard them; don't let them affect the culture. Sloppiness will lead to sloppiness or a lackadaisical attitude. The way the room is maintained will mirror how your program is maintained.

10

Using Technology in the Orchestra Classroom

Using Technology as an Integral Part of Instruction

When you think about playing classical music, modern technology doesn't immediately come to mind, but there are so many ways of using technology to help your orchestra. Unfortunately, technology is constantly changing so by the time you read this chapter there will be many new things that should've been included. This chapter will, however, attempt to inform orchestra directors of the many valuable technical tools currently available for use.

Before going out and spending money from your budget on the latest electronic gear, decide what you want to achieve by using the new technology. Some ways of using technology in the orchestra classroom will be to use it for recording and replay, tuning, listening to audio recordings, watching and making video recordings, video conferencing with guest artists who can't physically come into the classroom, and a host of other helpful activities. Here are a few suggestions for using technology in the orchestra classroom.

Recording Your Group

Probably the most valuable way to use technology in your classroom is recording your group. Recording your group for the best recording is more than putting one or two microphones in front of your group and pressing record. The object of making a recording is to give your students an opportunity to hear what you hear. The recording should be clear and balanced so that your students can critique themselves and understand what you've been talking about. You want them to hear the effects of sloppy attacks and releases and intonation problems.

If you have quality recording and playback equipment your students can hear what you have been telling them is good and what needs improvement. The book *Recording Tips for Music Educators* (Oxford University Press) goes into detail about different recording techniques and equipment that should be purchased and how to set up your equipment to get the best recording. This chapter will take a cursory look at a few ways to record in your classroom.

There are three basic setups for using microphones to record orchestras. The first is to use a parallel pair of microphones placed in front of the orchestra on a 15-foot microphone stand. The best microphones to use are condenser microphones with a cardioid pattern but a pair of dynamic microphones can also be used (see figure 10.1).

The next configuration is the X/Y pattern, also on a 15-foot stand placed directly behind the conductor facing down at the orchestra (see figure 10.2). Like the parallel pair, the X/Y setup provides a stereo pattern that imitates what the human ear hears.

The last of the three is used for larger orchestras. It's called the Decca Tree setup. The Decca Tree uses three microphones, one facing left, one facing center, and one facing right. You can also add two outlying microphones (one on each corner of the stage). Since you don't have three ears, the purpose of this setup is to give you a surround-sound effect that enables you to record every sound equally (see figure 10.3). Consult a recording professional for assistance with these setups and the best recording console to purchase.

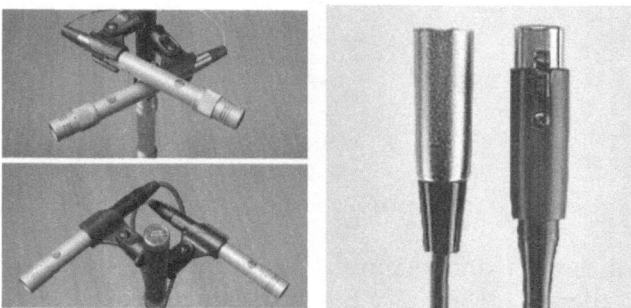

Figure 10.1. Recording setup. Courtesy of Shure Incorporated.

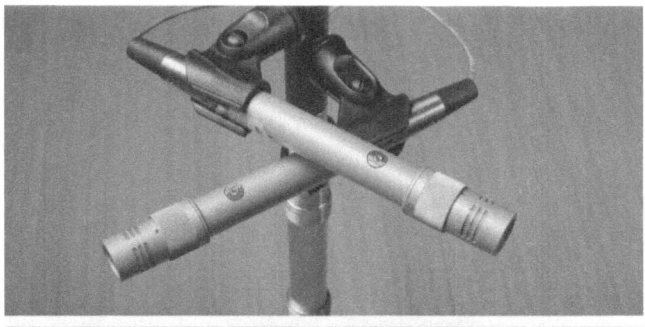
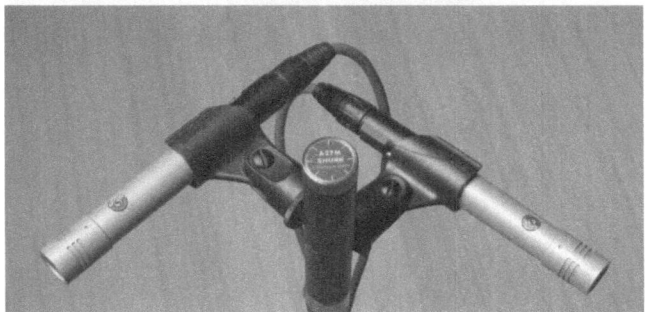

Figure 10.2. X/Y pattern with matching pair. Courtesy of Shure Incorporated.

Figure 10.3. Decca Tree. Courtesy of Paul Robinson.

If you don't want to purchase microphones and recording consoles, there's technology that can be used instead of microphones that can fit in your pocket. These devices are handheld recording devices (see figure 10.4).

Handheld recording devices have built-in microphones that can be configured into parallel patterns or X/Y patterns. The

Figure 10.4. Zoom X/Y and boom microphones. Courtesy of Zoom North America.

Using Technology in the Orchestra Classroom / 81

advantage of using handheld recording devices is that you can use free downloadable software to prepare your recording for replay for your students. Zoom, the leading manufacturer of handheld devices, makes microphones that can be used with iPhones and iPads (see figure 10.5).

You can play back your recording on any Bluetooth-compatible devices. The drop in quality from using microphones is slight but the advantage of handheld devices is that you can place them on a microphone stand in front of the group and get a representative recording for your group. A lot of smartphones and tablets have microphones for recording but the quality of the recording is not as high quality as microphones and handheld devices (unless you attach an external microphone or Zoom adapter microphone to them).

Some groups record with the idea of streaming their performances or formatting the recording to be sold. Before you

Figure 10.5. Zoom accessories. Courtesy of Zoom North America.

record and distribute recordings, you must secure the rights to record and distribute all of the music you plan to record. If you sell recordings with any copyrighted music that you don't have clearance for, you are in violation of US copyright laws. The Harry Fox Agency (HFA Songfile), ASCAP, and BMI have data bases you can search for publishing rights and secure permissions and clearances.

Using Tablets and Smartphones

Besides being able to use smartphones and tablets for recording, there are many other uses for them in orchestra classes. In a previous chapter it was discussed that smartphones and tablets can be used as chromatic tuners and metronomes. There are lots of tuning apps and metronome apps that can be downloaded for free. You should find the one best suited for your group's use and have your students download them for use.

Tablets and smartphones are handheld computers and give your students instant access to the internet. If you're preparing program notes on the pieces you're working on in class, you can have your students use a search engine to locate the information. This gives them valuable insight into the composer, the period, the style, and performance characteristics of the piece. Students are able to be active participants in the history of the piece(s) you've chosen. Orchestra students are generally some of the most academically advanced students in schools so engaging the creative and logical sides of their brains engages them completely.

Music on a Tablet

Many music publishers are currently making music available for download onto tablets. This helps to avoid torn or frayed music, lost music, and music too small for some students to see. Stage lighting is not an issue since tablet lighting can be adjusted to meet the players' needs. Another advantage of music on a tablet is that you and your students always have access to individual parts, there are no shared folders.

Leather-bound folders can be expensive and if a student loses the folder you have the expense of replacing the folder and all of the music contained in it. If a tablet is lost (an expensive loss), you can easily download the music onto another tablet. Smartphones can also download music but because of the size of the screen they are not practical for use during performances.

Interactive Software

One of the most used technologies in the band and orchestra classroom is SmartMusic. SmartMusic is an interactive music software program designed to go along with music instruction. Students receive immediate feedback on their playing and discover areas that need improvement. You can use SmartMusic for seating placement, playing tests, and practice monitoring. Students can learn scales, develop sight reading skills, and study the orchestra pieces you're working on in class. SmartMusic keeps students engaged in the learning process even when their part is not displayed.

SmartMusic is a web-based platform that has a huge library of music which enables you to create individualized lessons/assignments for every student. It provides a tuner, a metronome, practice exercises, and some of the requirements some states have for scales. The built-in notation tools allow teachers to create, edit, and import content for their students. Your students receive immediate feedback as they practice each assignment. You are able to receive their best performance of assignments so you can grade them.

With SmartMusic, the things discussed in the chapter about using smaller ensembles to help your orchestra can be done. Your students can work on specific assignments from you and submit their best work for you to grade.

Websites

The following websites are quite helpful for use in the orchestra classroom:

musictheory.net
musictechteacher.com
get-tuned.com
metronomeonline.com

Social Media

There are so many ways to use social media to work with your orchestra. All you need is a Bluetooth-enabled screen/monitor in your classroom. You can bring guest artists from anywhere in the world via Skype, Oovoo, or FaceTime. This real-time interaction allows you to have your students perform live for a clinician and get immediate feedback from them.

The guest can perform for your students so that they can model the sounds that they hear. Video conferencing can be done with a group of guests at one time so you can have every instrument in the orchestra represented in one session. Manufacturers like Conn-Selmer, Vandoren, and D'Addario have a list of performing artists who will come to your classroom via video conferencing or in person. Contact them or any other manufacturers to secure a professional who will demonstrate and interact with your group.

Facebook

Facebook has several groups dedicated to teaching orchestra and teaching music. Using Messenger, you can interact with orchestra teachers who can critique your orchestra and make valuable observations. The largest string teachers group is Orchestra Directors, but the Band Directors group (30,000 plus) has members who are going through the same pains you'll be going through as a band director teaching orchestra. You're not the first or only band teacher facing the challenge of teaching strings. Reach out for help when needed.

Twitter

Similar to Facebook, Twitter has members and groups that can be helpful to you and your students. You can keep up with new technology and find out which technology is best for you and your needs.

Google

Google has a number of things that can help educators. This search engine can help you find lesson plans and interactively engage with others in real time to customize lesson plans or get lesson ideas. Google Docs enables you to edit and write plans with several others in real time. YouTube is also a service from Google.

If you have a Gmail account you can easily sign in to Google. Everything is saved on Google Cloud. Students can submit written assignments to you for grading on a shared document (one student or a group of students). With Google Docs you can also create PowerPoint/Keynote presentations (Google Slides). This keeps students actively involved in the preparation of program notes and class discussions on music styles and music periods.

Notation Software

Notation software used in orchestra classrooms serves three major purposes, giving you the opportunity to rewrite or arrange parts for the group, allowing you to print missing parts provided by publishing companies, and allowing your students to compose and arrange. Music publishing companies have teamed with notation software companies to enable you to download and print parts you need from a huge database of songs. You may have to pay a minimal fee but if you've purchased the music some allow you to download a specified number of parts at no cost.

As is the case with using tablets, you have the option of printing or downloading onto the tablet directly. Sibelius and Finale are the two most used notation software programs but there are several available on the market to match your budget needs. It doesn't matter if you have a music store with a large inventory of music near you. All you need to do is go online and use a search engine to find the music you need. This is extremely helpful if you're in a rural school district. Going to state and national music conferences gives you an opportunity to keep up with current trends in music technology.

Giving your students an opportunity to create their own music or arrange music is another way of keeping them interested and actively involved.

Choosing the Best Notation Software for Your Program

When choosing notation software, there are some basic questions you need to ask:

1. Can inexperienced users use the program with a minimal amount of difficulty?
2. Will it satisfy the needs of advanced users?
3. Will the program allow you to extract and print individual parts?
4. Does it play back multiple parts or just a single part?
5. Will you be able to input dynamic and expression marks?
6. Will the parts automatically be lined up in measures, or will I have to do it manually?
7. How many parts can be saved if I'm writing or arranging a full score?
8. If I'm including transposable parts, will the program automatically transpose them?

9. Can I print professional-looking parts?
10. Will I be able to input lyrics if needed?

The answers to those questions will be used to decide on the software cost and how much of your budget will need to be allocated. If you purchase the software while you are building your program it is wise to purchase the software you expect to be using in your fifth year. Don't purchase something you will have to replace because your program has outgrown it.

Using Play-Along Software and Hardware

SmartMusic is not the only play-along software. There are other products that use the play-along function without giving your students a chance to record or submit to you for feedback or grading. These programs and hardware are just designed for your students to practice with.

There's available software that allows you to scan your score or their parts into your computer and have it automatically notated so that students may play along with it. Some will play the entire score with dynamics and expression markings while others will simply play the selected parts. There are those that allow students to slow the tempo down without affecting the pitch (those programs allow you to speed up the tempo, transpose the key, and loop difficult parts).

Some people think of play-along recordings just being used by individuals or small groups, but if you play them through your classroom audio system, your orchestra can play along with the recordings. You can even set the device on "loop" (repeat specific sections of the piece) so that you can work on specific problem areas. This enables you to move through the orchestra to give individual assistance to students who may be having problems that need your attention. Using SmartMusic in this way enables you to have the challenging parts appear on a screen so your students can read the music as they play.

The beauty of most technology for playing along is that they can be used together with very little effort. SmartMusic is an all-in-one package but most notation software can be matched with play-along programs to give the same or similar benefits (Sibelius and Finale have components similar to SmartMusic).

PowerPoint

Having students engaged in class rather than being an audience for a lecture is valuable. PowerPoint allows you to have interactive discussions so that students are active participants in the learning process (as was mentioned discussing Google Slides). Students are not passive learners having information given to them. As with using tablets and smartphones, students can see the information and digest it or ask questions that will stimulate the learning process.

You can combine playing and researching by including music to be played as stylistic and periodic information is given on screen. Google Docs, Evernote, and other systems allow multiple users to input information that can be disseminated or included in a single PowerPoint presentation.

Videotaping Your Orchestra

Just as PowerPoint is an important visual aid for teaching, videotaping your group can be a powerful tool. It combines the aural and visual elements needed for your students to evaluate their performance. As your students watch and listen to their performances and rehearsals, they will notice things that you cannot tell them to notice. Because most people are visually oriented, watching a video can be a much more valuable tool than listening alone. Guided viewing exercises are valuable and most digital video equipment uses digital stereo sound.

Zoom has a handheld device that combines digital audio recording along with high definition video recording. Earlier chapters discussed the importance of uniform bowing and visual stage presence and a video recording demonstrates the

Using Technology in the Orchestra Classroom / 89

importance of those details and how they affect the overall performance. During the guided viewing, before you comment on what you see, let your students voice their observations (see figure 10.6, a microphone adapter for an iPhone).

Another positive about visual effects is students will notice the importance of good posture, stand positioning, uniformity in dress, and looking up at the conductor. They've heard you talking about how important those things are but seeing them is worth a thousand words. You can also post the best videos on your social media pages and your website for others to see. Your

Figure 10.6. Zoom microphone adapter for recording videos. Courtesy of Zoom North America.

performances are valuable recruiting tools so make sure you only post what you and your students consider your best work.

Technology Resources on the Internet

Besides the pages listed earlier in the chapter, here are some more sites that are useful:

www.smartmusic.com
www.sweetwater.com
www.soundtree.com
www.ti-me.org
www.finalemusic.com
www.nafme.org
www.sibelius.com
www.avid.com

Maintenance and Record-Keeping

For basic program maintenance there are programs that can be kept on your computer, tablet, or smartphone for you to keep accurate inventory, music library information, financial records, and other records in one place. This keeps you from having to have file cabinets filled with records and enables you to instantly call up needed information wherever you are. If your group is away from school and you need student health records or other pertinent information, simply pull it up on any mobile device. Charms and Filemaker are the two most preferred but there are plenty of others that are made for non-performance classes that can be adapted for your use.

Charms Office Assistant can organize your library, track your inventory, equipment, medical forms, and outfits if they're owned by the school. It also helps you keep up with your boosters' finances, giving parents an opportunity to pay for trips and other bills with credit or debit cards (it has a parent/student/

member area). You're able to use it to keep up with practice logs, audition materials, pictures, and other items important to the life of your program. Having Charms or any other management program frees up your time to devote to teaching music.

Technology Resources in Book Form

Burns, Robby. 2016. *Digital Tips for Music Teachers*, New York: Oxford University Press.
Hamann, Donald L. and Gillespie, Robert. 2018. *Strategies for Teaching Strings*, 4th ed., New York: Oxford University Press.
Kearns, Ronald E. 2011. *Quick Reference for Band Directors*, Lanham, MD: Rowman & Littlefield Education Publishing.
Kearns, Ronald E. 2017. *Recording Tips for Music Educators*, New York: Oxford University Press.
Rudolph, T. E. 2004. *Teaching Music with Technology*, 2nd ed., Wincote, PA: Technology Institute for Music Educators.
Turner, Cynthia Johnston 2013. *Another Perspective*, Reston, VA: National Association for Music Education.

Chapter at a Glance

Unfortunately, teaching orchestra classes in the twenty-first century is not that different from teaching orchestra in the nineteenth or twentieth centuries in some schools. There is so much technology available to you now that can make teaching orchestra classes more interesting and engaging for your students. *Teaching Music* magazine and *Music Educators Journal* and other periodicals have product reviews and recommendations that fit the needs of the twenty-first-century classroom. Going to music conferences on the state and national levels will also keep you up on current trends in music education. The adage "work smarter, not harder" applies here.

11

Using Small Ensembles to Improve Your Orchestra's Sound

Small Ensembles

As stated earlier in the book, there will be three kinds of students in your program—highly proficient, proficient, and below proficiency. The largest percentage of students will be in the proficient range. These are the students you will base the level of your class literature on. The most at-risk students will be in the highly proficient and below proficient range.

The highly proficient students are at-risk because they can get bored or lose interest while you try to teach the rest of the class. The below proficient group will be at-risk because they will struggle to keep up with the class. Using small ensembles and solos will help you reach both at-risk groups (using SmartMusic is a good solution to this problem).

Being able to use small ensembles to improve the overall performance level of your orchestra is a valuable tool for many reasons. Because small string ensembles are reduced orchestras, they enable your students to put to use all of the skills required for good orchestral playing. The smaller group helps students hear the importance of accurate bowing, balance, intonation, attacks and releases, rhythmic accuracy, and many other orchestra playing skills. Sonata allegro form for a string quartet is exactly the same as Sonata allegro form for a full orchestra.

Not being distracted by several instruments playing helps students concentrate on the skills they need to accurately implement the skills you're expecting them to apply in the larger group. They can apply these skills as they concentrate on playing their parts accurately. The subtle way they are learning these valuable techniques enables them to naturally apply them and internalize them.

Since there is generally no conductor in small ensembles, members are forced to listen to the other parts that are being played along with theirs. You don't have to match players with equal performance skills with one another. In fact, it's sometimes better to have highly proficient first violin players play with players of lower skill levels. This transfers to listening for and matching the concertmaster in the orchestral setting. It also helps to keep lower level players from being intimidated in the larger setting (when seating your orchestra, the second best violin should be principal second violin).

Your state's solo/ensemble list will provide a good starting point for music selection. As with selecting literature for the larger group, the literature you select should be challenging but not overwhelming. The main goal is to give your students a meaningful experience that will easily be transferred into the larger orchestra setting. When students play in a string quartet, one person not playing their part well negatively impacts the group. Students subconsciously realize the importance of their part and generally work hard not to let the group down.

Small ensemble playing does not have to be limited to homogeneous instruments. You can match your stronger string players with your strong wind players. This will help keep your strong string players from getting bored and it also helps develop their listening skills. You can use some of the Brandenburg Concerti for this purpose. Because Bach wrote the concerti for instruments he had available at the time, you can use them for mixed ensembles and challenge your top band players and top string players. Doing this helps you lay the foundation for a full orchestra.

If you check your state's solo/ensemble list you can find literature written for most combinations you want to put together. Even if you need to write substitute parts you will be able to accomplish your goal of keeping all of your top students engaged. The idea of selecting music that will stimulate and challenge your students is the goal. Program one of the ensembles on one of your concerts to motivate your students to work hard in the small ensemble rehearsals.

The teamwork and camaraderie developed in these small groups will transfer to your larger group. You're establishing "study groups" for your orchestra and providing your students with a group of people they'll be comfortable practicing with. If you discover some of your top players getting bored as you work with problem areas in the music, release them with their quartet or octet to go work on the music. As stated in the Technology chapter (10), they can submit their work to you via SmartMusic.

If you don't have enough students to go to the orchestra festival/assessment, choose literature for solo/ensemble festivals from the list and let the ensembles go for adjudication. Solo and Ensemble festivals are not competitive and you can choose to receive comments only to help your students hear what an objective ear thinks about your work and your students' achievements. Criteria such as attacks and releases, intonation, bowing, dynamics, and sound quality will be judged. Since these are things you will be spending time on in class, having an adjudicator evaluate your group will reinforce the importance of accuracy in performance.

Once again, string ensembles are like miniature orchestras, the same principles of good orchestra playing apply to smaller ensembles. Accuracy in performance is expected. The ratings for small ensembles are the same as for orchestra—Superior (I), Excellent (II), Good (III), Fair (IV), and Poor (V). These ratings are designed for orchestra directors to use as teaching tools and are the same for full orchestra.

Using Solos to Keep Your Best Players Interested in Staying

Just as small ensembles help students stay engaged and encouraged, solo playing is a valuable tool for maintaining students.

In your first year of orchestra, you're going to have a mix of highly proficient and self-motivated players and students who you will constantly monitor for motivation and interest. Soloists participating in solo/ensemble festivals will not be restricted by the grade level of classroom music.

Your most advanced players will be given an opportunity to play music that's a challenging level you may not be able to introduce to the full orchestra. You can give them an opportunity to practice their solo piece during class time while you work on passages that your orchestra needs repetitive work on if you have a practice room available (play-along and SmartMusic). Once again, boredom is the biggest cause of students dropping out of orchestra. Besides small ensembles, solos are a valuable tool for challenging and retaining students.

Assigning solos to students is also a way to encourage your students to take private lessons. There will be things as a band director that you won't know about individual performance techniques that a string teacher will know. Your higher level students will need to receive these skills from a string performer. Because this is such an important part of your orchestra development, at the beginning of the school year, you should provide your students and their parents with a list of private teachers.

As you compile the list, you can ask the teachers to give you their rates for thirty minute, forty-five minute, and sixty-minute lessons. Students should be encouraged to take weekly or bi-weekly lessons based on the lesson length and/or the location of the private teacher. Include this information in your handbook and on your web page so parents have access to it all year. If possible, in the early years of your teaching, invite the private teachers to come to your school for coaching sectionals or side by side playing during class time (Skype lessons work well for this).

Your parent group may help defray the costs of having these specialists come to the school for coaching. If several students want to take lessons from the private coach, the coach may reduce their price. Depending on your fundraising efforts, the cost of coaching may be included in your annual operating budget. Some large programs engage adjunct faculty members from local colleges or universities to regularly come in during class time to coach students. Students tend to share information they have received with students or sections that have not received coaching. Especially in your early years, having specialized clinicians come in to work with your students is invaluable.

Basic Small-Ensemble Playing

Just like in your full orchestra, eye contact in the smaller setting of a trio, quartet, quintet, septet, or octet reinforces the need to watch other players as they plan for accurate entrances. Attacks must be precise and can easily be heard if they are not. Obviously, with fewer players your students will hear the discrepancies more easily, but once their ears have been trained for listening, the skills can be transferred to the larger setting. A sloppy attack or release will be a lot less difficult to hear in the smaller ensemble than in the larger group, but the impact is the same on both groups.

The most important things you want to train in smaller settings are listening and watching. Listening is important because it will control precision, intonation, balance, rhythmic accuracy, and expression. The visuals are bow positioning on the string, bowing length, attacks (articulations), and bow placement (close to the bridge or away from the bridge), and in the larger setting, watching the conductor. Students will learn to use their peripheral vision to see and match bowing.

Depending on the size of your orchestra, peripheral vision may or may not work well. This is where developing good cross-listening skills is needed. The exercises used in the chapter on lesson plans are good for ear development. Have your players do scale exercises with their eyes closed. This forces them to use their aural abilities over their visual abilities.

In the smaller ensemble you can teach some of the nuances that are difficult to teach in the larger ensemble. Skills such as playing close to the fingerboard for softer playing or playing closer to the bridge for louder playing can be demonstrated better in the smaller setting. Videotaping the smaller groups helps students see and hear how bow placement and bow pressure affect sound volume and sound production.

The subtleties of vibrato are easier to see and hear with smaller groups. Once again, if you allow the small ensemble to practice during class time, having them record their work on SmartMusic and send it to you for review helps to keep them focused.

Chapter at a Glance

Having chamber groups can be helpful in developing musicianship in your orchestra. Intonation, bowing, attacks, and releases can be learned in small groups and expanded to the larger group. Working with smaller groups will also help you develop the comfort level of your lower achieving students. Having your principal players work in a string quartet will give you an opportunity to observe string playing close up.

Students helping students has proven to be a very effective way of building confidence and learning new skills. Students who help other students with the learning process internalize the skills they're teaching. In small ensembles students use the same skills and techniques they need for larger ensembles with the added effect of team building.

Appendix A

INVENTORY FORM

Instrument _____ Brand _____
Instrument Serial Number _____ Model Number _____
Year of Purchase _____
Condition _____
Finish _____ (with or without lacquer)

Permission Slip (Local)

Student's name _____

Activity _____

Activity date and time _____
(periods/classes missed)

I give _____ permission to ride school provided transportation to _____ with the orchestra on _____ (date)

I do not give _____ permission to participate in this activity. I realize this is a graded activity and my child will be penalized for not participating.

I give _____ permission to participate but I will transport him/her to and from the activity.

I give _____ permission to participate in the above named activity and go in parent/adult driven transportation.

Signed _____ Date _____

Permission Slip For An Out of Town Trip

Student's Name _____

Activity Name and Date _____

Parent's Name _____

Parent's Phone _____

I give _____ permission to travel out of town with the orchestra

_____ (date). Signed _____ Date_____

MEDICAL FORM

Student's Name _____
Parents' Names _____
Parent's Phone Number _____
Parent's E-mail _____

Student's Medical Condition _____ (Good, Fair or Poor)

Does the student have any medical condition that requires attention _____
    If yes, please explain _____

Does the student have any food allergies or special dietary concerns? _____
    If yes, please list and explain _____

Glossary

Arco: Play with the bow.
Articulation: The way in which a note or phrase is attacked
Bow direction: A series of symbols that indicate whether the hand pulls the bow downward to the right, or upward to the left.
Bridge: A piece of wood that stands on the body of the instrument and that supports the strings and transmits vibration.
Brush stroke: An off-the-string short note where the bow is lifted at the end of the note.
Con sordino: With mute.
Contact point: The part of the bow that touches the string to produce optimum sound.
Détaché: Separate bowing but full note value.
Frog: The lower part of the bow.
Glissando: A slide upward or downward between two or more notes.
Jeté: "Throwing" the bow. The performer skips or bounces the bow across the strings to create fast arpeggios.
Legato: Smooth, elongated bowing to connect notes.
Marcato: Emphasized accents, with marked emphasis.
Martelé: "Hammered" bowstroke in which a musician uses a sharp accent with each note.
Martellato: A hammering of a note using the upper bow.

Pizzicato: Plucking the strings with the right hand while the thumb is balanced against the fingerboard.
Portamento: An audible slide from one position to the next.
Ricochet: Fast bow bounces.
Saltato: Same as ricochet; throwing or bouncing the bow to play several notes.
Sforzando: Suddenly loud; with sudden emphasis.
Slur: An articulation symbolized by a curved line, above or under, which connects the notes smoothly.
Spiccato: A short and detached note played by bouncing the bow.
Staccato: Short and detached.
Subito: A sudden change in dynamics.
Sul tasto: Playing over the fingerboard.
Tenuto: Note held for full value until the attack of the next note.
Tip: The upper part of the bow.
Tremolo: A technique of multiple up and down bows as indicated by the composer.
Trill: Rapid alteration between two notes, usually by step or a semitone apart.
Vibrato: The variation in pitch by the finger, hand, or arm to provide warmth to a note.

References

Burns, Robby. 2016. *Digital Tips for Music Teachers*. New York: Oxford University Press.

Consortium of National Arts Education Associations. 1994. Reston, VA: National Standards for Arts Education.

Hamann, Donald L. and Gillespie, Robert. 2018. *Strategies for Teaching Strings*, 4th ed. New York: Oxford University Press.

Kearns, Ronald E. 2011. *Quick Reference for Band Directors*. Lanham, MD: Rowman & Littlefield Education Publishing.

Kearns, Ronald E. 2017. *Recording Tips for Music Educators*. New York: Oxford University Press.

Rudolph, T. E. 2004. *Teaching Music with Technology*, 2nd ed. Wincote, PA: Technology Institute for Music Educators.

Turner, Cynthia Johnston 2013. *Another Perspective*. Reston, VA: National Association for Music Education.

Index

adjudication: by students, 67–68; teaching for, 62–64
adjudicators. *See* judges
advanced players, challenging, 42–43, 95–96
apps, for tuning and metronome, 30, 82, 83
articulations: for bowing, 62; as period accurate, 44, 66; for wind players, 5
assessments. *See* festival performance
attacks and releases: in ensemble playing, 97–98; for string and wind playing, 5, 10, 33–34
aural discrimination, for tune, 30
awards, with orchestra program, 20, 23, 73–74

Bach, 17, 29–31, 94
Back to School Night, 25, 39
band directors, 1, 3, 20, 84–85, 96
band students contrasted with string students, 1–2, 40
bass vibrato, 12

baton, students watching, 32–33, 34
"big thing," in rehearsal, 44
booster groups. *See* support network
bounce bowing, 5–6, 9–10
bow: curve, 10; lesson plan for, 28–29; placement, 5; playing without, 8, *9*; pressure, 10
bowing, *8*; articulations for, 62; first rehearsal instruction, 44; intonation of, 29–30; lesson plan sample for, 28–29; martele, 11; music parts marked for, 66; off-string and on-string, 6; playing without, 8, *9*; pressure of, 10–12; ricochet (saltato/saltando) and, 9–10; techniques for, 1, 6, 7, 30–33; videotaping of, 88
bow parts: frog, 4, 5, *8*, 29, *32*; grip, 4, *5*; middle, 8, *8*, 29; tip, 4, 6, *8*, 29
Brandenburg Concerti (Bach), 17, 94

bridge position, 72
brush stroke, 6

cello, vibrato, 12
challenging: advanced players, 42–43, 95–96; rhythms as, 65
Charms Office Assistant, 90–91
Chorale (Bach), 29–31
chromatic digital tuner, 30
class, 17, 18, 43–44; microphone recording in, 78; performance in, 20, 27; room maintenance for, 72–73, 75; syllabus, 19–20, 25–26; technology tools for, 77–91
"close," not enough for orchestra, 28
community diversity, 22
composers, suggested, 45–46
concert: attire for, 23, 58–59; rest position for, 56
concertmaster, 29, 33, 56, 57, 66
conductor, 57; students watching, 32–33, 34
confidence: building, 12; in selling yourself, 13
copyright laws, US, 82
crescendo and decrescendo, 65–66
cross-listening, 29, 33, 43, 97

Decca Tree. *See* microphone
détaché, 6
digital tuning apps, 30
diminuendo. *See* crescendo and decrescendo
director, band, 1, 3, 20, 84–85, 96
distribution: of orchestra handbook, 25; of performance recordings, 82

ensemble playing, 1, 93–95, 97–98
equipment: budget for, 16, 39, 40; maintaining, 69–73; repairs, 71
etude (warmup scale), 32
exercises, 11, 33, 34; of scale, 97; for team building, 42
expectations: for classroom and performances, 26; managing, 17–18; for orchestral students, 21
expenses, of orchestral programs, 21, 23
experience level, of students, 14, 42, 54, 93
extracurricular orchestral music program, 20–21

Facebook, 84–86
fate of music in schools, 14
fees and expenses, 21, 23. *See also* equipment
festival performance: grades and ratings for, 61–64, 67–68; participation in, 20, 24; period accurate articulations, 66; playbook for, 64–67; Solo/Ensemble festivals and, 95–97; teaching music for, 63–64
Finale notation software, 86, 88
finances. *See* fundraising
finger placement: for attack, 33–34; pad *vs.* tip, 11; pizzicato and, 8, 9; for vibrato, 10–12
first rehearsal: classroom management during, 42, 43–44, 45; music for, 41–42, 64; no "little things" in, 44; planning, 17–18. *See also* rehearsal
five-year plan, orchestral program, 15, 69–70, 74–75

flying spiccato (*jéte lent*), 9, *9*
frog, of bow, 4, *5, 8,* 29, *32*
full bow *vs.* half bow, 44
fundraising, 16, 21, 23–24, 35; financial officer for, 36; parents for, 39; recordkeeping, 37–38, 90–91

Google, 85
grades and ratings: festivals/ assessments and, 61–62; policy for, 19–20, 24–25, 26
grande détaché, 6
grip, of bow, 4, *5*
G. Schirmer Inc., 29

half bow vs, full bow, 44
handbook, orchestra, 19–21, 22–26
handheld devices, *80, 81,* 88–89
hand vibrato. *See* wrist
hardware, for play-along, 87–88
homework, 17, 20

individual recognition and praise, 73–74
instruments, 1, 3–4, 16, 21; carrying, 57; storage for, 72–73
interactive software, 83, 88
internet resources, 90
intonation, 27, 28, 29–30

jéte lént (flying spiccato), 9, *9*
judges, 59, 62, 67–68

laws, copyright, 82
leadership team, 36–38
legato, 6
lesson plan, 15, 17, 27, 45; attacks and releases sample for, 33–34; for festivals/assessments, 64–67
lesson plans, sample: bowing, 28–29; conductor and baton watching, 32–33, 34; intonation for, 29–30; tempo control, 30–33
lesson plans, writing, 27–28, 29–34
lessons, private, 96
levels: of experience, 14, 42, 54, 93; of performance, 41–43
listening skills, 29, 33, 97–98
literature, for orchestra, 41–47, *48–51,* 53–55

maintenance and purchases, 69–73, *72–73, 75,* 90–91
management: of classroom, 17, 43–44; of time, 17
marcato, 6
martelé, 6, 11
martellato, 6
Megavox (Bluetooth amplifier), 31
melodic lines, 54, 65
metronome, 31, 82, 83
microphones, 78–83, *79, 80, 81, 89*
middle, of bow, 6, *8,* 29
mission, of orchestra: support network for, 16, 35–40; teaching, 14
mission statement, 14, 25; orchestral program description, 22; of performing groups, 15–16
model behavior, student, 17
multiple note playing, 9–10
music, 58, 82–84; educational role of, 14, 15; melodic lines

in, 54, 65; selecting, 41–42, 54, 64, 94; style and period of, 44; suggestions for, 48–51; supervisor of, 20–21; transcribing, 42–43
musical periods, 41
music appreciation, 14–15
Music Booster Manual (NAfME), 35
music education: five year plan for, 15–16; philosophy of, 14–15, 18, 25, 75
music supervisor, 20, 21
music value, educational and instructional, 41

National Association for Music Education (NAfME), 15, 24, 25, 35
network, of support: bylaws of, 37–38; creating, 15–16, 35–40; leadership for, 36–40
notation software, 85–87

off-string and on-string bowing: multiple notes through, 9–10; techniques of, 6, 7
orchestra: literature for, 41–47, 48–51, 53–55; participation rules for, 21; progress evaluation of, 24; sections taught together in, 64; support networks for, 16, 35–40; teaching, 1–4; technology in, 77–91; tuning, 43
orchestra handbook, 19–26; on concert attire, 23, 58–59; on festivals/assessments, 61; private teachers list in, 96; on trips, 20, 21, 23, 38

orchestral music program, 1, 15, 22; awards for, 20, 23, 73–74; building, 13–14; "close" not good enough for, 28; festivals and, 24; five-year plan for, 15, 69–70, 74–75; maintenance and growth of, 69–75; requirements, expectations and cost of, 21, 23
orchestra students, 3–4; band students contrasted with, 1–2, 40; expectations for, 21; recruiting, 13–14
orchestra support network, 16, 35–36; committees of, 37–40; fundraising through, 24, 39
orchestra teachers, 1, 2, 4
orchestra websites, 21, 84, 90
"our program," 18, 22

pairing students: for rehearsal, 43; for small ensembles, 93–95
parents: leadership of, 16, 22, 35–40; meeting, 16, 25, 39
pedagogy, string, 1, 3
"people resources," 37
percussion instruments, 3
performances, 23, 53–57; accuracy of, 44; attainable level of, 41–43; in class, 20, 27; expectations of, 26; guided listening evaluations of, 20, 67; judges of, 59, 62; music folder for, 58; participation in, 20, 24; recording for, 82; streaming, 81. *See also* festival performance
performing artists, by video conference, 84
periods, musical, 41, 44, 66

personal: contact with students, 13; mission, 15; statements of teacher, 20, 25
philosophy, of music education, 14–15, 18, 20, 25–26, 75
phrase shapes, 65–66
pizzicato, finger positions for, 8, *9*
planning: festival performance, 61; lessons, 17, 27–28, 34; rehearsal, 17–18, 43; units, 28
play-along, software and hardware, 87–88
playbook, for festival performance, 64–67
plucking (pizzicato), 8, *9*
position: of bridge, *72*; concert rest, 56
PowerPoint, 88
pressure, bow, 5, 10, 11
private coaching and clinicians, 96–97
programs, string, 13–15, 22, 69–70, 90–91
publicity committee, 37–40, 74
publicity/social media advertising, 39–40
publishers, suggested, 46–47

quartet, string, 94, 98

recognition and praise, 73–74
recording and playback: copyright laws for, 82; of rehearsals, 67–68; technology for, 78–83, *79*, *80*
record keeping, for program, 37–38, 90–91
recruiting: program for, 69–70; publicity/social media for, 39; by students, 13, 16; with website video, 89–90
rehearsal, 17–18, 20, 43; "big thing" in, 44; first, 41–42, 44; lesson plan for, 27; no "little things" in, 44; pacing for, 66–67; recording, 67–68; suggestions for, 46–51
releases, of string notes, 33–34. *See also* attacks and releases
repairs, equipment, 71
resources, 15, 37, 90, 91. *See also* technology
ricochet (saltato/saltando), 9–10
rushing momentum, fighting, 30–40

saltato/saltando (ricochet), 9–10
scale, musical: exercises of, 97; for warmup, 32
seating, 33, 55–56
selecting, music, 41–42, 54, 64, 94
selling: copyright laws and, 82; orchestral music program, 13; recording and, 81; yourself, 13
sfortzando, 6
shareholders: meet with, 16; of orchestral music program, 15; "our program" with, 18, 22
Sibelius notation software, 86, 88
site reading, 64
16 Bach Chorales (G. Schirmer), 29
skill levels, 42, 55
small ensemble, 93–95, 97–98
SmartMusic, 26, 83, 87–88, 93, 95–96, 98
smartphone, 82, 88, 90
social media, 84–85
social media committee, 37–40, 74
software, 83, 85–88

Solo and Ensemble festivals, 95–97
Sonata Allegro form, 93
spiccato string note, 6, *8*
staccato string note, 6
storage for instruments, 72–73
streaming performances, 81
string instruments, 1, 3–4, 10–12
string pedagogy, 1, 3
string program, building, 13–14
string sections: ensemble for, 95; instruments of, 1, 3–4, 10–12; methods for, 5–6, 46–47; pedagogy of, 1, 3; quartet for, 94, 98. *See also* programs, string
string students contrasted with band students, 1–2, 40
students: achievements of, 18; as adjudicators, 67–68; behavior of, 17; class performance of, 20; experience level of, 14, 42, 54, 93; fees assessed to, 23; first performance activities of, 54–55; judging by, 67–68; learning from each other, 43; listening skills of, 29, 33, 97–98; mission statement amended by, 22; music for development of, 14; of orchestra, 3–4; orchestra benefitting, 13–14; personal contact with, 13; preparation of, 63–64; reclaiming, 16, 70; recognition and praise for, 73–74; recruiting by, 13, 16; string contrasted with band, 1–2, 40; teacher bond with, 2; types of, 93; videotaping performances of, 88–89
style and period of music, 44
subito (sudden change) *vs.* gradual change, 66

"supporting roles" award, 74
support network, 24, 58, 90; creating, 15–16, 35–40; leadership of, 36–38; of parents, 16, 35–40
syllabus, class, 19–20, 25–26

tablets, 82–83, 86, 88, 90
teachers: confidence in, 12; of orchestra, 1, 2, 4; personal statements of, 20, 25; private, 96; students bond with, 2
teaching, 4, 14; for adjudication, 63–64; of demonstrations, 11–12; from Facebook groups, 84–86; orchestra sections together, 64; visual aids for, 88–90
technology, in classroom, 77–91
tempo, 30–33, 87–88
tenuto notes (full value notes), 6, 66
terminology, 1, 2, 12
testimonials from students, 16
"tick track," 31
tip, of bow, 4, 6, *8*, 29
"top heavy," violins, 42, 44
transcribing music, 42–43
tremolo string note, 6
trips, of orchestra program, 20, 21, 23, 38
tuning: apps for, 30, 82; with Concertmaster, 57; by cross-listening, 29, 33, 43, 97; first chair violin player and, 43; with get-tuned.com, 84; process of, 29, 43
Twitter, 85

uniformity: of attire, 23, 58–59; of music folder, 58
United States (US) copyright laws, 82

unit plans, 28
unit tests, 20
"unsung hero" award, 74
US. *See* United States

vibrato (rocking) bow note, 10–11; of cello and bass, 12
video conference, with performers, 84
videos, instructional, 11–12
videotaping performances, 88–89
violins, "top heavy," 42, 44

warmup (etude), 32, 44
watching: of baton and conductor, 32–33, 34; other students, 97–98

websites: for orchestral programs, 21, 84, 90; video recruiting tools of, 89–90
whole note / full bow, 34
wind instruments, 3; airflow through, 1
wind notes, 6; attacking, 5
wrist: exercises for, 11; vibrato for, 10–12
writing lesson plans, 27–34

X/Y microphone pattern, *79, 80,* 80–81

YouTube, 3, 11

Zoom microphones, *80,* 81, *81,* 88–89, *89*

About the Author

Ronald E. Kearns is an author, educator, record producer, and performing artist. He was a band, orchestra, and jazz ensemble director for thirty years in public schools in Maryland. He has produced more than forty recordings for commercial release, including six of his own. During his time teaching, his groups won numerous Grammy Signature Schools awards, and Ron was honored by *SBO Magazine* and *DownBeat Magazine* for excellence in teaching.

Ron has written several articles on jazz, music production, and music education and is the author of the books *Quick Reference for Band Directors* and *Recording Tips for Music Educators*, which are being used as textbooks for band directors and music educators at colleges and universities across the United States. He is a Vandoren of Paris Performing Artist, a Conn-Selmer Endorsing Artist, and writes articles for Vandoren's website.

www.ingramcontent.com/pod-product-compliance
Lightning Source LLC
Chambersburg PA
CBHW030145240426
43672CB00005B/271